THIRD PARTY

IN

MARRIAGE

PASTOR
ADE OKONRENDE

THIRD PARTY IN MARRIAGE
Author: Pastor Ade Okonrende.
First Edition— January 2019

Contact: Pastor Ade Okonrende.
Email: okonrende@aol.com
Phone: 832 723 8470, 832 .372.0860

Inspiration: Holy Spirit

Chief Editor: Choice Okonrende

Cover design: Gfaydesigns
www.gfaydesigns.com 832.623.1201

Pagination and layout: Pastor Christy Ogbeide.
Christyogbeidebooks.com 832-661-4352

Books by the author are available at:
choiceworldpublishers.com
Amazon.com and leading bookshops

Printed in the United States of America

All scripture quotations are from the King James Version of the Holy Bible, or the Amplified Bible unless otherwise stated.

DEDICATION

This book is dedicated to the glory of God in appreciation of my wife, Pastor Grace Modupe Iponwonsa Okonrende née Imafidon.

She had been of great support from the inception of our marriage. Her endurance of the boredom created by my writing, especially in the bedroom had been the source of joy and solution to the challenges in the marriages of others. I salute your tolerance of "THE SECOND WIFE" [As my Writing has been branded.] On your permission, this has come to stay. I guarantee your pleasure shall forever be treasured.

Thank you for your sacrifice to humanity and better marital relationships.

APPRECIATION

I acknowledge my fathers in the Lord.

Rev. G.O. Farombi, [Foursquare Gospel Church Nigeria] my very first pastor in the Gospel. A general who forever 'refires' never to retire. Now setting the system on the Holy Ghost fire in Chicago, USA.

Pastor W. F. Kumuyi, [Deeper Christian Life Ministries] my campus and literature pastor.

Pastor Rufus Owoade [Formally of Foursquare Gospel Church Ita-Iyalode, Abeokuta, Nigeria. Now the General Overseer of Disciples Gospel Mission. 33, Elite Road Idi-aba Abeokuta, Nigeria.] Who launched me into ministry.

Pastor E. A. Adeboye my father and mentor who discipled me through the Christ the Redeemer Ministries and the basis of my membership of the Redeemed Christian Church of God.

I acknowledge your individual contributions to my attainments in the ministry. May the Lord strengthen you all that you may finish well and strong.

I write to appreciate our children: Grace, Chosen, Choice and Royal who have made us proud parents on many instances. I pray that you will not be victims of third party trauma and tantrums. In Jesus mighty name.

I sincerely appreciate the contributions of my committed friends and "Children" in the Lord who proofread and contributed to the final finish of the entire work: Sis. Sade Olakehinde, Sis. Oyindamola

Adeosun, Bro. Chinedu Obeleagu and Pastor Mrs. Tokunbo Daniel of RCCG Open Heavens Parish in the Republic of Ireland.

I especially appreciate Rev. Val George, who did a tremendous work, she proofread and also wrote the foreword to this book.

The success story will not be complete without the mention of the wonderful contributions of my very committed Associate pastor: Dr. Christy Ogbeide, a versatile writer and publisher who did the pagination of this book with utmost zeal. She has been a "bridge".

Finally my sincere appreciation goes to our son, Choice Okonrende, a 2018 graduate of English language from the famous Houston Baptist University, Houston Texas USA. He took the publishing of this book as the second product of his publishing house: Choice World Publishers Inc. I admire your courage and tolerance of my resistance to your corrections and rephrasing of some of my expressions which I fought hard to retain as I desired. Thank you for allowing some of them to remain.

FOREWORD

Every married couple, Christian and non-Christian alike, come into marriage with a truckload of baggage. Young and veteran couples today face many challenges. Regardless of age or creed, God still holds couples accountable for the sanctity of marriage.

In the past decades, nuclear family structure had steadily been on the decline because of political and ever changing socio-cultural values. All these changes contribute to the struggles of married couples to survive or have a semblance of marital bliss. The pressures of daily living: what to wear or eat, where to live and how to survive additions to the 'load.' Time management is a major area of challenges for marriages. Families juggle schedules to match up with the daily challenges and basic chores. All these invariably serve as inanimate third parties in marriages.

"Third Party in Marriage" is a book meant for such a time as this. It intends to redefine the image of any individual, group or organization due to the power of its influence. On a broader perspective, "A third-party in a marriage is a person, animal, plant, habit, object or subject that infringes on the relationship of the married couple or prospective marriage partners.

Pastor Ade continues to win bragging rights on successfully learning how to navigate through third party influences in his marriage. Married for over thirty five years (and still counting), Pastors Ade and Grace Okonrende are an inspiration and gift to the Body of

Christ. The lessons in the narratives in this book add sanctity to marriage. With the insight God has given him in his marriage, "Third Party in Marriage" is quite engaging and entertaining. The book is down to earth and practical in its approach to examining challenges couples face. The gems of wisdom and suspense in the pages will keep a reader engrossed.

Pastor's Ade dogged desire to enrich the Body of Christ has taken him on this journey of discovering new insights to what would make marriage have an edge over other human endeavors. His story as a husband and renowned author will be inspiring as the years go by. He has successfully made excellence the aspiration of many in his generation. The impact of his writings will surely be justified by posterity. I recommend that this impacting and entertaining piece of work, be read by all to enhance our daily walk with God. Couples will be enriched by the basic principles gleaned. With its captivating play on words, comprehensible dialogue, every chapter has all the ingredients of a full 'five course dinner' in one. At every turn of the page, you encounter new characters with unique third-party issues. This is about leaving a legacy of love, long lasting values that remind couples of the reason they got married in the first place.

This book is launching a new wave for Christians who are confident in making their marriages a living witness to the goodness and glory of the Lord. According to an author, "Well fed fish do not need the bait offered by a fisherman." This book also serves as a warning bell and cautionary note to seasoned, matured and new marriages. Every marriage has its giants or third parties. This book opens the heart of readers to understanding how to combat these giants. It is necessary to know that you are not alone in this journey.

The storms the characters in this book faced and weathered will equip every reader to scale through the third-party challenges in marriage.

Val George
Author, Licensed: Daily Practices into a close
Relationship with God.

TABLE OF CONTENTS

PREFACE

Third party is defined as a third person or organization less directly involved in an activity or in a legal case than the main people or organizations that are involved. (The Cambridge Advanced Learner's Dictionary & Thesaurus)

We shall however in the circumstance of a marital relationship view a third-party at a broader perspective. A third-party in a marriage is a person, animal, plant, object or subject that infringes on the relationship of the married couple or prospective marriage partners. A third party could therefore be animate, inanimate, visible, invisible or supernatural. A third-party could be a person, parents, siblings, in-laws, pets, habits, practices, lifestyle, career or any obsession. There is no doubt that the inanimate or abstracts are functionally real especially in marriage relationship. Third party may redefine the image of an individual, group or organization due to the power of its influence. These third parties, if allowed, will fester and cause marriages to become loveless, truncate destinies, cause disunity that could spell separation and irreparable damage. Please realize that you are accountable to God and your spouse.

Every married person desires personal relation-ship with his or her spouse. There is always the desire for a sense of ownership and undivided personal intimacy with the partner. Reactions to the activities of a third-party are determined by the temperamental disposition of the individuals involved in the relationship. It is a hidden fact that a third party that is always glossed over is the invisible dominant "force" that rules the life of any individual. An example of this force is what psychologists call: Temperament. This is the true invisible but noticeable image of an individual. This force is responsible for the action, reaction or inaction of the individual. It is in control but may always be unknown. This defining force determines the fate of other third-parties. Whether visible, invisible or invincible, a third party is a force that has influence on a relationship outside of the desires and in some cases beyond the control of the parties involved. When it comes to the issues of third party in a marital relationship, there is more to it than meets the eyes. Please realize that danger could not be more dangerous than the ignorance of its existence.

CHAPTER ONE

THE UNKNOWN SPOUSE

The temperamental disposition of your spouse will remain an invisible third party until you master it. Your mastery does not make the relationship itch free. Anyone who does not know his or her personal temperamental disposition or have an idea of the disposition of his or her spouse will invariably have to contend with the individual's temperamental disposition as an "unknown third-party." Very few things could be more frustrating than living with someone you do not know, who speaks a language you do not understand and your tastes are at variance.

TEMPERAMENTAL DISPOSITION: AN INVISIBLE THIRD-PARTY [culled from: Ade Okonrende-"Understanding your Spouse"].

The study on human behavior that analyzes the factors responsible for action or reaction as determined by the mind and mental state of an individual is simply referred to as psychology.

The study on temperament is the analysis of human or animal nature or behavioral pattern as is peculiar to an individual. An individual's temperamental disposition determines his or her character trait, personality makeup, mindset, which is responsible for the individual's action, reaction or inaction.

When an individual comes under the control of his or her temperamental weakness, the manifestation may throw any observer off balance. Psychologists have categorized human temperamental dispositions under the following: Choleric, Melancholic, Sanguine, Phlegmatic and Supine. The supine character is the modern "Jack of all trade" who, strangely masters many of the skills.

Every individual's disposition is determined by the dominant trait. No one is absolutely 100% of a particular temperamental trait. An individual is an embodiment of two or more traits, the dominant and mild may vary in percentages: 60/40, 90/10, 55/45, 70/30. Those who have equal percentages of two dominant traits are very prone to mood swings and are not easily predictable. Most people with Supine dispositions fall into this category.

An attempt will be made to give insights to the peculiarities of each of these temperamental dispositions. Here, more emphasis will be laid on the weaknesses of the dispositions because the weaknesses are principally responsible for the rifts in relationships. No one hates the advantages in life but the disadvantages. For a matrimonial bliss please carefully read about the dispositions and analyze your experience of your partner and the understanding you have of yourself.

THE CHOLERIC

The Choleric personality is a powerful character that can be a wonderful asset to the spouse and the entire community if properly handled. The strength of the choleric can be likened to that of a unicorn. It could run itself to death and may not be concerned about others in the pursuit of its desired goal. The choleric is self-driven, self-confident with the flare of superiority and extraordinary ability to achieve the desired goals. He/she justifies personal weaknesses and views others as the cause of his or her personal errors. He/she takes pride in personal obstinacy, a trait assumed to be the springboard of his/her past victories. An average choleric is very stubborn and opinionated, believes he/she is always right. Personal ability is highly treasured and believes in independence. The opinions of others are relegated except when he/she gets into serious trouble, for which he/she blames others. The choleric is domineering, wants to lead, take the first place and have the last say. In his/her inordinate ambition, others are belittled and in most cases combated. The choleric feels deeply hurt when not able to have his/her way. The choleric vehemently resists every resistance and very prone to making offensive remarks that are carefully crafted to make him/her sound decent, polite but yet damaging to the emotion of the objector. The choleric in his/her impetuous anger may exaggerate and misconstrue the intentions of others and pervert the words of those who oppose his/her view. The choleric may ruin a relationship or investment he/she has taken years to build. The pride of the choleric makes apologizing a difficult task. Deceit, disguise, hypocrisy and placating the opposition are exploited as escape routes. The choleric may not be sentimental, sympathetic or romantic. He/She is a goal-getter, this makes it difficult for him/her to realize her offenses against others. However the choleric has a lot of good to offer.

THE MELANCHOLIC

The melancholic person is not easily excited or impressed by whatever acts upon him /her. His/her reaction is weak but holds to the impression or his opinion for a long time. A repeat of whatever forms the bases of his/her impression makes him/her come to a level of almost irreversible opinion about the circumstance or individual. The melancholic is a deep thinker. He/she reflects more about his/her experience or impression. The melancholic is compliant, adherent, but has almost zero tolerance for any noncompliance of people around him/her. He/she may be easily excited, impressed or disappointed but will successfully conceal his/her impression which forms the bases of his/her opinion of the affected. The melancholic does not feel comfortable in a crowd, he/she is a lover of solitude which is a solace for his/her weakness of being easily distracted. A melancholic has a very serious mind and looks at life from that angle, they can be very pessimistic and have great fear of failure. This is responsible for his/her careful preparation for his/her limited risks and accepted challenges. The melancholic is a passive personality without the active propensity of the choleric. Very sluggish and indecisive but very resolute and tenacious when he/she eventually takes a decision. Always trustworthy but finds it difficult to easily trust others, yet easily taken in by others as he/she expects everybody to be trust worthy. This forms the bases of his/her lack of trust when dealing with others. The melancholic is slow and awkward, a trait he/she considers a necessity for his/her avoidance of error or failure. He/she is a slow worker, a pessimist that views himself /herself as an objective optimist. To him/her, being slow implies carefulness. He/she does not seek honor or recognition, not due to humility but the fear of humiliation or disgrace. A melancholic may have the best to offer but may not make known his/her ingenuity or potentials until compelled to perform. A melancholic is always a good benefactor to humanity.

THE SANGUINE

The sanguine is an "effervescent personality", very vivacious and enthusiastic. He/she is easily impressed or excited but the impression is but for a moment. He/she is an extrovert, fun lover, a party person and possibly a talkative. A sanguine is in most cases very superficial. He or she does not take things or situations very seriously. In most cases his/her impression does not stand the test of time. He /she is easily distracted or attracted to a "new thing" The sanguine in most cases is unstable and unreliable in his/her decisions. He/she easily finds a reason to respond to an appeal for/to change. This instability is responsible for the flirty life of the sanguine. He/she can be very fickle. He/she may stand to oppose what he/she previously defended. A sanguine may quickly or easily pass from tear to laughter or vice versa. Very unreliable, not very dependable. His/her love for variety is responsible for the proneness to infidelity. The sanguine is an optimistic person who does not brood on his/her failures. His/her strong inclination for vanity and self-complacency is evident in his/her craze for good appearance, flattery and high impression by others. Could be easily suspicious and jealous of his/her spouse as he/she falls a victim of finding in others what he/she hates in him/herself.

The cheerfulness and inordinate love of pleasure of the sanguine leads him/her into frivolity. Mortification is a big problem to the sanguine. His/her eyes and taste may always go out of control and may always be a victim of "verbal diarrhea"[revealing or divulging confidential information]. The sanguine disposition makes most wrong decisions when compared with other temperaments because his/her sense of judgement is very superficial. The sanguine has higher records of failure because he/she takes success for granted. He/she can easily be misled because of his/her lack of personal convictions on his/her line of action. The fact remains that the sanguine is easier to pacify at the moments of conflicts as he/she could easily turn a new leaf to suit the occasion.

THE PHLEGMATIC

The phlegmatic is a weaker version of the melancholic with minor variables. He/she is weak in action or reaction and may not at all be touched by impressions. He /she is not worried about the opinion or impressions of others. A very slow person who prefers repose and leisure to the strain of labor. A phlegmatic person may be very negligent of others or duties. He/she does not display the vicissitude to lofty heights of the choleric but very reliable to commitments. Very inclined to ease, eating and leisure. He/she may be the best of brains, has the best ideas but never manifest knowledge until the final moments when he/she is called upon to perform. The phlegmatic excels averagely above his/her contemporaries in tasks or duties he/she chooses to perform. May not always be pushy but very resourceful in the field of his/her excellence. An introvert, silent at group discussions, quiet over issues that would have erupted or incurred the anger of the choleric. An average phlegmatic may not easily respond to offenses but could be resolute in final decisions.

THE SUPINE

The supine disposition may be an embodiment of virtually all of the other four temperaments at varying or equal percentages. The supine is very unpredictable but very effective in multiple activities or tasks. A supine character is a goal getter in his/her areas of interest. Works well on personal conviction in compliance with instructions or the laid down principles. Prefers to work alone under the instruction of a trusted leader. He /she have a servant heart. Would put in his/her best for the desired result in the interest of others, they are emotional and affectionate but lacks the ability to express their desires. They expect others to be able to read their mind. An average supine desires a person he/she can depend or rely upon for trust and reassurance of confidence and love. They lack the ability to initiate or truly express love yet are trustworthy lovers. They need constant reassurance that they are loved and appreciated. A supine may not express love or emotion until he/she feels safe to do so. He/she senses the need for affection and love but finds it difficult to express. Desires passionate relationship and deep affection but lacks the initiative. Finds it hard to speak his/her mind. Can be very emotional, may run tap-of-tears when emotionally abused. A supine may be very confused after listening to many opinions and may not be able to express his/her personal conviction or what he/she wanted. To the supine, exclusion is seen as rejection. The supine is always referred to as "natural born victims" because in his/her attempt to serve or please others at his/her detriment may feel unappreciated. Though a Supine may manifest some of the choleric traits but contrary to the choleric, the supine is not self-opinionated, in most cases lacks personal confidence and seeks the opinion and the endorsement of others. He/she broods and cries over his/her greatest frustrations, disappointments and lack of appreciation.

APPRAISAL

Please appraise yourself and your partner. A fair appraisal/assessment will give you an insight to how your relationship can work better. Please realize that in practical criticism, you see first in others what you hate in yourself. If you realize some peculiarities of your spouse or yourself, please work on them to the advantage of you both. Do not attempt to condemn but rather commend. An individual in most cases may not act or react contrary to his/her temperamental disposition except under the influence of the Holy-Spirit or any other supernatural force

It is a natural tendency for dogs to bark or bite. It will be an abomination for a monkey not to be able to jump or climb. The grunting and squeal of the pigs are normal and natural tendencies. It is a difficult task to stop the goat from bleating or the lion from roaring. Do not condemn your partner for being real, according to his/her temperamental disposition. Please take time to discuss your observations or realization so that you both will be on the same page and will be able to resolve issues amicably.

The greatest modification to any individual's temperamental disposition will be determined by his/her PERSONAL RELATIONSHIP WITH THE HOLY-SPIRIT.

Please realize that little or no emphasis was laid or mentioned about the good qualities or advantages of the various temperaments. They all have their strengths. Until you know and master your temperamental disposition and that of your partner, this invisible third-party will remain the ruler of your life and relationship. Many who never realized the power of this third-party make comments such as, "I don't know what else to do to make this marriage or relationship work". For further reading on temperament.

CHAPTER TWO

THE ABSTRACT THIRD-PARTY

Whatever is said to be abstract may only exist in thoughts or as an idea but may not have a physical concrete existence to the knowledge of all. It could be said to be theoretical, conceptual, metaphysical, philosophical or notional but yet has a very powerful influence on the actions, reactions or inactions of an individual. As defined, an abstract third-party may not be obviously visible but evidently influential on the decisions of an individual. It may have to do with an obsession or an ambition that has taken possession of the individual. The fact remains that a possessive ambition rules and could ruin the life of its possessor. An abstract third-party could be a set of goals by an individual in diverse aspects of life whether academic, career or desired material attainment. It could be very obsessive and possessive. Desired accomplishments determine the response of the affected individual to most issues.

CAREER OR OBSESSION

Education was the most cherished asset and preoccupation of Zach. To him, whatever obstructed his studies was an enemy of progress. At thirty five years old he was in pursuit of his third PhD program. His classmates call him 'bookworm'. His parents pressurized him on the issue of marriage, they were scared that he was becoming a "professional student." Marriage was not his priority but he could not stand the emotional stress of his father or the agonizing tears of his mother. He had no choice but to agree to get married before he was forty years old. He was not the choice of many ladies because they were scared of his indifference to human emotions. A lady who declined his conjugal proposal referred to him as "married-to-books." She claimed she would not want to be a second wife. It was a big relief for Zach and his parents when Angelina agreed to marry him. Angelina was once a student in one of the universities where Zach was a lecturer. She loved his academic ambition and aspirations. She was an unknown mentee that had derived inspiration and obsession for academics due to the influence of Zach. Their love story began when they met at a seminar where they both were speakers. Most of those who knew them well enough claimed that they both were going into their second marriages respectively as they were both initially married to books. The wedding was moderately solemnized. They both enjoyed their privacies and academic obsessions. They were a couple to be reckoned with in the academic circles. They got a lot of grants and sponsorships for their research works. They were able to break new ground in their respective fields. Angelina was not bothered about having a baby. She had many books to take care of. Her mother put her under a great pressure on the issue of giving her at least one or two grandchildren.

Zach loved his mother-in-law for the fact that she assisted on convincing his wife to get pregnant, a desire that had been declined and obstructed through effective family planning device. They had a "compensational" pregnancy. She was carrying a set of twins. The pregnancy was a little traumatic as Angelina was about to hit her fortieth birthday. She hated her mother and her husband for what she called an obstruction to her career and destruction of her elegant curves and beauty. There was no doubt that pregnancy did not favor her. She looked like a caricature of her true self. The babies came out a boy and a girl. She felt satisfied believing henceforth the gates are closed against prospective pregnancies. The two children looked exactly like their father. They were very dark in their pigmentation. They were described by somebody as "doubly-baked at the time they were created." Arrangements were made to bring Angelina's mother into their home to help babysit the twins as the care for them was too stressful for their mother. It did not take long before their relationship experienced some challenges. Grandma Pedro, was of the opinion that she should be paid for her services as a babysitter of her grandchildren. Angelina could not agree with the idea of her mother giving them terms and conditions for her services. Zach had no problem with the idea but would prefer that same offer be granted to a complete stranger who preferably did not snore as loud as Grandma Pedro did. According to Zach, "her pipe organ" disturbed him at study and obstructed his concentration. Angelina was used to her mother's "membership of the choir" while asleep. She claimed she was not happy with her mother's proposals but still felt safer entrusting her children to her mother to babysit.

Zach felt his mother-in-law was an obstruction and disturbance to his career. He could not find a better solution to the scenario than to stay away in his office to do his studies. This was the beginning of a strain in their relationship. Grandma Pedro felt bad that her son-in-law stayed away from home because of her. She schooled her daughter against her husband. She would on many occasions question her daughter whether she was sure that her husband was not having affairs with other women as he claimed to be in his study at the University. With time the idea was nursed by Angelina, she determined to monitor her husband to be sure that there was no act of infidelity. She questioned her husband a series of times on what happened in his office when he was there alone. Zach initially did not attach much importance to her curiosity until she actually insinuated that he must have found a new lover. Zach responded like it was a silly joke, "I have kept the same lover that I had before getting married to you." With a smile he turned around to embrace the love of his heart but was shrugged off like a plague. It was his first time of experiencing a turn-off from his wife. He questioned the reasons for her unfriendly attitudes. "Come back home" she responded with a frown. "Your mother is the repelling factor. If I stay home to study, I will turn out to be a failure because your mother snores too loud." Angelina was offended. She said, "I guess we need to bring your mother in to do this job." "If that be your resolve, my mother will surely do it at no cost," he responded with an enigmatic smile. She went into her mother's room and informed her that her husband wanted her out because he wanted to bring his mother in. Grandma Pedro incidentally overheard their discussions. She looked straight into her daughter's face as she said, "I knew from the beginning that you were not happy to meet my terms and conditions for babysitting your children. If your mother-in-law will do it for free, get her in and kick me out. Your husband's excuse of my snoring loudly is a good reason for him to go back to his old time lover. Please inform him that I am not the cause of his infidelity. I will no doubt leave your home and go back to my husband who has been of great endurance for the safety of your children..." Angelina was speechless. She never anticipated such an outburst from her mother. Looking away from her mother as she walked out of her room she said, "I am disappointed, I guess I will have to talk to Dad about this development." "Your Dad was aware of your plan to enslave me from day one of this issue. He will happily receive his wife back with joy. She picked up her phone and pointed it to Angelina to call her Dad. It was on this note that Zach strolled into the room. Grandma Pedro did not allow him to say a word before she charged at him, "If I were your mother, you would send me out of your home because I snore? When you bring your own mother in, make sure that you stop her from breathing when she sleeps so that you can read your books for which you have no time for your wife and children. I guess by then you would not have any excuse to see your former lover."

Zach turned and looked at his wife in the eyes as if to ask, "what is going on?" Angelina knew that her mother misconstrued her husband's reference to his academic addiction when he said, *"I have kept the same lover that I had before getting married to you."* She made a sign to pacify him to overlook the errors and tantrums of her mother. Zach walked away quietly without any response to the statements of his mother-in-law. Grandma Pedro determined to ruin any chance of Zach's mother, Grandma Briggs from accepting the proposal of her babysitting for Angelina. She decided to attack Grandma Briggs on the issue. She told her on phone that she had seen her plans hatched on how to take over her position. She said, "You have done well to push me out of your son's house, but remember his wife is my daughter. I just want to appeal to you that you do not give my daughter any horror when you achieve your desired goal." Grandma Briggs had no clue to her allusions. She questioned her on what exactly she was trying to put across. Grandma Pedro dropped the phone on her. She told her daughter she was ready to leave. She would not listen to any plea. She packed her little belongings and moved out of the house. Her daughter pleaded to no avail. Zach's voice was an irritant that sent her whining. Angelina's phone rang, it was a call from her sister-in-law, Mrs. Cecilia Washington the younger sister of Zach. She called to know exactly what was going on as her mother had narrated to her, her ordeal with Grandma Pedro. Angelina was shocked that her mother had gone that far. She realized that her mother was in the wrong but would not want to own up. Instead, she questioned her sister-in-law on why she was the one that called on the behalf of her mother. She said, "I am not exactly sure of what is actually going on. However I do not expect you to call on behalf of Grandma." Her concluding remark was offensive to Cecilia. She felt insulted because she was a little older than Angelina. She reported her experience to her mother. Grandma Briggs never would expect any offensive remark from Angelina because they had always being in good rapport. She told her daughter not to take offense from Angelina's snobbish attitude. In her own words, "Angelina must be passing through some challenges if she was not reacting based on occasional feminine hormonal imbalance. She had always been my wonderful daughter-in-law." She determined to call Angelina on the phone. Angelina received her call and responded very pleasantly. There was no trait of any contention, misconception or domestic friction. Grandma Briggs was shocked to have been given such a reception when in her understanding something had gone wrong along the line in the relationships. At this juncture, Grandma Briggs narrated her experience with Grandma Pedro. She realized that her mother was doing everything to make it impossible for Grandma Briggs to accept the proposal of her coming to stay with them for the care of the twins. She pleaded with her mother-in-law to forgive her mother. She tried to convince her to come over to stay with them. Grandma Briggs informed her daughter-in-law that the proposal would cause disaffection in the extended family. She counseled her to find a neutral person in their local church or neighborhood to take the job.

Angelina and her husband were disappointed by the decision of Grandma Briggs. Zach pleaded to no avail, his mother tried to explain to his understanding why it was not proper for her to come over to take care of the toddler twins. Zach claimed that her decline will make his wife hate her mother the more. With a smile she said, "The conflict between a child and his/her mother will eventually be resolved, it is I that should not get into any conflict with your wife. I got the message of her mother. She doesn't want me to come to stay with you. My decision is to let peace and sanity reign." Nodding his head in acknowledgement of the wisdom in his mother's decision, he requested that his mother should recommend someone to whom she could entrust her grandchildren. "The request is good but it should not come from you. Leave that to your wife. If the idea is initiated by her, she will be able to defend it before her mother," she asserted. "But she is not in good terms with her mother, he inferred. His mother laughed as she said, "Don't ever make the mistake of you being sandwiched between your wife and her parents, especially her mother." Zach took a deep breath. Looking straight into his mother's eyes, "thank you for this tutorial, you have successfully tilted my line of reasoning in the right direction. We shall surely get someone of her choice." Cecilia Washington was still brooding over Angelina's response to her call. She purposed in her heart to discredit her in the sight of her brother.

A surprise fortieth birthday party was organized in honor of Angelina. The party was well attended but Cecilia was conspicuously absent. Her brother was worried that she did not attend the birthday party of her assumed friend. He had always known them as being in good rapport. He did not attribute her absence to any misconception on the issues of the Grandmas. He called her on the phone in attempt to get her to speak to her assumed friend. After the usual courtesy greetings he proposed giving the handset to the celebrant, the move was declined by Cecilia. He asked for the reason for her decline. She replied, "Please say me well to her that should be good enough." Zach was very displeased by her outright decline to have a conversation with Angelina. He decided he would never call her until she called him. As he was about to hang up he said, "Please call when you are ready to talk to Angelina. Cecilia got the message right but she was adamant on not speaking to her Sister-in-law.

Months went by and there was no conversation between Zach and his younger sister Cecilia. She did not send any seasonal greeting card throughout the year. When no card was exchanged between them both at Christmas, it became obvious that the gap had degenerated into a rift. Zach was more uncomfortable with the setting of things between his wife and his parents, especially his only sister. He decided to visit his parents in company of his wife and children on one of the national holidays. His wife declined the proposal. She said she would not get to see Cecilia at the family house except she tendered an apology for her absence at her fortieth birthday celebration. In Zach's perspective, the reason sounded too trivial to create such a rift in the family. He felt angry but realized it was not a time to apply force or be adamant on the issue. He pleaded to no avail. In his frustration he proposed an alternative, which was to visit the parents of his wife. She declined his proposal with the notion that her mother would play hostile due to the decision to have her out of their home. Indignation was about to take over Zach's emotion. He remembered the popular slogan of his Pastor, "When you are angry, learn to borrow smiles from the Holy Spirit." He smiled at his wife as he said, "Ok! Choose a place for us to spend the brief public holiday." "Home!" she snarled. "Not this time around, we must go somewhere. I have given you the options. If you would not accept any of them and will not suggest one, I will decide for you," he said affirmatively. "And you will carry me on your head," she retorted. Zach was literally deflated. He almost blew his top. He excused himself from the room. Angelina got the message, she knew her husband had become outrageously angry. She knew walking away was his style to avert his emotional outburst. The phone rang and it was a call from Angelina's uncle who happened to be in a business partnership with Cecilia Washington. After the exchange of pleasantries, Zach was better composed, and his anger had subsided. He reluctantly asked Mr. Regent about his plans for the coming public holiday. With excitement Mr. Regent invited Zach and his family to join them as they were going to host some friends and family members. Angelina was excited to join the team of her uncle for the get-together. The day came and they all headed in the direction of the Regents.

Their will rolled the wheels in their desired direction. It was a full house. Many friends, family members and business partners were present but Cecilia Washington. Angelina was particularly happy that Cecilia was not at the meeting. She was at liberty, as free as the roach in the sewer. Her husband had never seen his wife as expressive as she was at the get-together. He was excited and very happy for her. Suddenly there was an eclipse which was prompted by the unexpected appearance of Cecilia who stormed into the gathering with great excitement. Almost all present were familiar with her. The meeting was a reunion between her and some of the guests. She was busting and bustling into everybody. Angelina stylishly took her exit before Cecilia came in her direction. Her sudden withdrawal was too obvious to most observers. Zach watched the scenario with a very heavy heart. He determined to use the occasion to reconcile his sister and his wife. He went after his wife, pulled her to himself and said, "I guess it is time for us to head in the direction of my parent's or your parent's house." Angelina realized that her husband was being sarcastic as probable reasons for her action was evidently understood. He tried to kiss her just to burst the bubble of animosity and hatred. She turned away, but he successfully whispered to her ear, "Please forgive in your own interest. You cannot drink poison and expect your 'enemy' to die. Why would the sudden appearance of someone rob you of your pleasures and companionship." He observed that her eyes were glazed with tears that were about to roll down her cheeks. With the palm of his hand he wiped her face and the tears wet his palm as she burst into hooting and howling. He curdled his wife and assured her that she would be reconciled with her one time friend and sister-in-law.

They were quite away from the crowd. Hardly could anyone decipher the cacophony. Cecilia instinctively walked towards her brother before she realized that Angelina was shielded off by him. She stopped abruptly but her brother signaled to her to come closer. Angelina raised her head up only to discover that her offender was close by. Though the tears were dried up but her eyes were still red and evident of pain. Cecilia moved very close to her one time friend and said, "Let's bury the hatchet, I still love you irrespective of the offense. If you bled, I feel I bled more. I have had sleepless nights in acknowledging the pains. I am happy we met for this awesome moment of reconciliation. Please forgive me. If you wronged me, I guess I wronged you more. Please let's stop the venom before it kills us." It was a wonderful moment of reconciliation. Zach rounded off the reconciliation by reminding them of one of the profound statements of their pastor, "Offenders may die but offenses don't. Please let us kill the offenses now before they kill us." Angelina pulled her sister-in-law to herself, they had a beautiful embrace for the first time in about three years.

Zach was very happy that his sister and his wife were friends again. He felt hypocritical for holding his mother-in-law guilty of attempted matrimonial disorder. Though he did not vent his pain or acknowledgement of the offense, he knew that his love for her had diminished. He had not given her any surprising but conventional gift since the incident occurred. His wife observed it but it was difficult for her to mention it because her husband never spoke or made a reference to the offense. She knew her husband did not talk fondly about her mother as he would normally do but it was difficult for her to open the chapter. She was surprised when her husband expressed his intention to visit her mother with a surprising gift. She was sure it was the first of its kind in three years. He knew her mother-in-law to be a little high handed and could be forceful on some issues that ought to have been glossed over. He prayed for divine favor before his mother-in-law. Angelina had a burning desire to make the trip with her husband, she was a little apprehensive of what her mother could do. However she opted out because she was not feeling fine. She had visited her primary physician without any clue to her challenges. It was agreed that Zach should go with the twins and their nurse.

The absence of Angelina must have been a divine arrangement as it got her mother a little agitated. The meeting was a good moment of reconciliation. Grandma Pedro was anxious to know the state of her daughter. She was assured that she was fine. Zach did his best to convince her that her daughter was doing well. His conclusive statement was that the primary physician was yet to know the cause of her intermittent nausea and loss of appetite. Grandma Pedro was very worried, she decided to call her on the phone. Angelina did not sound too excited to talk to her mother. She still held her guilty of seeking monetary reward to take care of her grandchildren. She could not get over all her instigations and insinuations that could have disrupted her marriage if not destroyed her home. She remembered vividly her mother's strategy to prevent her mother-in-law from coming to babysit for her. She was hesitant to explain her feelings or symptoms.

The experienced grandmother, Mrs. Pedro, could not hold back her impression. She advised her daughter to take a pregnancy test. Angelina was angered by this. She cautioned her mother never to mention the issue of pregnancy. She claimed she was the one who pestered her into getting pregnant which resulted to the birth of the twins. Her mother calmly responded, "I thank God I did not talk you into this. Please go back to your doctor or buy a pregnancy test kit to at least get to know what exactly in going on." She again warned her mother never to suggest that she was pregnant. She jokingly said, "Even Grandma Briggs who once asked me whether I was going to remain at 'a draw', never pestered me or suggested that I am pregnant. She told me I started with twins, the next may be triplets. That is why I have determined never to get pregnant again." "Ok, I wish you are not pregnant but please go and test for pregnancy. If you are, they will be the babies of Grandma Briggs and I will readily babysit them for free." Her mother jokingly promised. Zach was again well pleased with the discussion between Angelina and her mother. He told his mother-in-law, "I wish she is pregnant. It will be my greatest joy. My mother said most women who set out with a set of twins are in most cases so blessed with multiple egg production at ovulation and may always give birth in multiple." His mother-in-law cut in to assure him of every support if it turned out that the weakness was a 'blessing'. "I will personally be ready to count the weeks and come over to nurse your ambition." "I guess I am not ready for triplets." Zach pleaded. "Let's wait till the test is done." They both laughed. It was a good time of reconciliation. Zach returned home with joy. Angelina was very happy for the reunion between her husband and her mother.

Zach was of the opinion that the pregnancy test was necessary because the doctor had not been able to clearly confirm the nature of the illness. He decided to drive the car straight to the clinic. He declined the proposal of his wife to buy pregnancy test kit. The doctor conducted the test and confirmed that Angelina was about three weeks pregnant. She screamed, "NOOOOOOO Not me, it's not going to happen. Noooooooo." The doctor was surprised at her reaction. He turned to her husband and asked whether he would want him to suck the fetus out. According to him it was just like a blood clot. Zach turned to his wife and asked whether she would want the fetus sucked out. "You mean to kill? I said it did not happen." Angelina snarled back at her husband. "It has happened already," he gently affirmed. "I guess it is your desire to ruin my career and turn me into a nanny". "I didn't do the family planning, you did." "But you refused to do the vasectomy I requested that you do. You are the cause of this mess," she screamed with tears. "May God forgive you for your ingratitude," Zach prayed. "I didn't ask God for this, so you can't make me feel sorry. Now I know you wanted it. Your mother demanded for it. Now you have it. If you have it your mother's way, I guess you will have to look for additional jobs to afford a bigger house," she retorted. Zach was quiet when he thought of the possibility of the theory propounded by his mother. His wife looked at him with all seriousness and could sense his sobriety. She said, "I am in this already, there is no sucking out. I refuse to be a murderer. Just pray your mother is a false prophet, if not, you are in for a nursery home." Zach looked dumbfounded as if waiting for the doctor's second opinion. They headed home.

Angelina started putting things together for the coming baby. She determined not to discuss with either her mother or her mother-in-law. She told her husband, "You will be the one to tell the world what you did, "You are the 'causer'." Zach was not excited about the whole development and couldn't help laughing when he remembered the story that surrounded the statement, "You are the causer."

At the ultrasound test it was confirmed that Angelina was carrying a set of triplet, all boys. They were both silent. She looked at her husband snobbishly with disdain. He felt offended but could not express it. He did not know what to say. After a while he said, "what shall we do." "LIKE HOW! You are in for it already. Your mother is not a false prophet but you will pay the price for her prophecy," she asserted. He was very sober. It was obvious he was overwhelmed by the thought of the responsibilities ahead of him. He said, "I guess it is time to tell the old ladies what they both desired." Looking melancholic, Zach pleaded with his wife to please understand that he got more than he desired. Cuddling her he said, "Please do not lose sight of the 'God factor' in this issue. We did not plan it. God must have His master plan that we cannot see now due to our academic exuberance and obsessions." Angelina was silent, she was not pleased with the comment of her husband and at same time not ready to conflict with the issue of the God factor. In a very low tone she said, "I am not happy with the way you are bringing God into what happened. We would have been safe if you did the vasectomy." He took offense in what he saw as an attempt by his wife to indict him for the pregnancy. He was silent briefly before he walked out of the room. She knew her husband was seriously offended. She knew his solace was in silence in order to get over his boiling anger which he had always successfully concealed in his pride. She knew it was not time to aggravate him by pushing the issue any further. She felt bad that she incurred his concealed anger. She desired to walk her way back into his pleasure without missing out on her attempts to make him feel her pain over the unexpected pregnancy. She would not want to tender any apology for expressing her disappointment over the pregnancy. Suddenly it dawned on her that there were many women who desired to be pregnant for just a child but never could. She hooted with tears rolling down her cheeks. Her husband rushed into the room, he was scared with the imagination that his wife must have suffered an emotional breakdown. It was a big relief when he realized that she was convicted of the sin of ingratitude. On a more serious note, he was happy that she was convicted by the Holy Spirit. He stylishly embraced her as she threw herself into his arms. She wanted his affection and acceptance. It was her way of tendering her apology for forcing him to feel guilty. It was a good moment for them both to express their desires for affection and acceptance. It was a very romantic moment that ended up in thrilling sexual intimacy. Angelina still in the frenzy of the moment said to her husband, "I guess you will not run out of town if what you just did increases the number to six. I have resigned myself to fate. We can successfully launch the baby factory. You may be surprised to realize that this is the best sex I've had since we got married in my opinion. I had no fear of any pregnancy. I am delivered from the spirit of fear forever." "You have successfully passed the fear to me. We must do something drastic if you want your deliverance to be permanent without having to pray any deliverance for me over the spirit of fear," her husband responded.

"Drastic, like what?" She asked. "Hysterectomy, of course. That is the most secure for a person like you where pregnancy may cut corners and beat human imagination," he replied. "No, this time around, we're both going in. I will have tubal ligation while you get a vasectomy. If they removed my uterus then I would be on medication for a long time," she asserted. "That is fine," he concord.

Angelina was successfully delivered of the three bouncing baby boys. It was a height of celebration in the extended family but pity in the academic circle. The naming ceremony attracted donations and gifts from various quarters. Many of their colleagues were curious to know how they planned to take good care of the five children with the close age range between the first and second batch. It was time for Grandma Pedro to keep her promise. She was actually willing but Zach would not want her to come back because of her propensity of intrusions into their private life. However clever and stylish he was on the issue, his decline was obviously connected to the past experience. Grandma Briggs was scared of the aggression of her rival Grandma Pedro. It was eventually resolved that a distant relative of Zach should be granted a solace in their home while she was separated from her husband due to violence and abuse. Everything was right until a sudden rivalry developed between Theodora and Angelina. Theodora was a little younger than Angelina but their culture demanded that she be accorded some respect by Angelina because all relatives of the husband were expected to be treated with a measure of respect. Their relationship was supposed to be symbiotic, Angelina needed a babysitter while her sister-in-law needed accommodation. There was no negotiation on remuneration. Angelina felt they were doing her a favor while Theodora felt she was being taken advantage of. The Cold War continued until Angelina felt it was not safe to keep her children at the mercies of her sister-in-law. It was difficult for them to negotiate on a basic allowance. Angelina wanted Theodora out of the home but her husband was insensitive to the Cold War between the two ladies in his house. Theodora was visited by a man she described as a distant cousin not known to Zach. Angela thought the guy was dating her. The suspicion became obvious and the relationship got more strained. Angelina became desperate about getting rid of Theodora, but her husband wanted her to remain because of her free babysitting service. The crack in the home degenerated into a gap that worsened into a rift which almost ruined their marriage. It was resolved that Theodora should leave, a decision that did not go well with Zach's parents. His mother adjudged

Angelina's mom as the brain behind the conflict between her two daughter-in-laws. The exit of Theodora was a challenge as they desperately needed a full time baby sitter so that Angelina could continue with her job in the University. Her most preferred person was her mother-in-law, but it was difficult to engage her because Grandma Pedro never gave up on her desire to come back. She had in the process charged both her daughter and her husband that their Christian practice was defective because they did not completely forgive the past. Her allegation was refuted by her son-in-law on the grounds that he did not want her to come back because he was trying to protect the relationship between them both.

Angelina desperately wanted her mother-in-law to settle with her family to take care of the children. Her husband eventually suggested that her mother should come along, a suggestion he made to ward-off the move of his wife. Strangely his wife responded, "If that be the basis on which your mom would come, let the two of them be with us. At least accommodation is not the problem now that the university has given us a bigger house." Zach was not comfortable with the idea of bringing his mother and his mother-in-law under his roof. He stylishly cautioned his wife on the proposal but she was bent on having her mother-in-law around to take care of her children. Zach knew he had a big lump to swallow and an Herculean task to convince his mother to come stay with them while his mother-in-law was around. He pleaded with his mother that she should accept the proposal because he would not want his wife to feel she was indifferent to her plight. Grandma Briggs agreed to do all things to please her son and his wife. Things worked out and the two old ladies had a room each to them selves. Grandma Pedro was a strong choleric that would not accept correction from anybody in the house. She had a lot of very offensive dirty habits. During her first stay the defects were not too obvious because her daughter was always bridging the gap.

Angelina was of the opinion that she did not have to keep her eyes on the issue in the house because she had her mothers with her. The untidiness of Grandma Pedro was concealed until Grandma Briggs decided she would no longer go the extra mile to keep the home tidy. It became obvious that things were gradually getting out of hand. No one could talk to Grandma Pedro except Angelina. Zach was hesitant to tell his wife about the dirty habits of her mother. No one spoke about her snoring any longer. On a particular occasion Angelina confronted her mother on a batch of plates left in the sink. Incidentally they were briefly put in the sink by her mother-in-law while she dashed to meet the needs of the triplets. The issue became a very bad fracas as grandma Pedro flared up at her daughter, "I knew it that you have been made to believe I am the pig in this house. I guess you need to find out who did the mess this time around. Angelina was greatly offended by the reaction of her mother. She said, "I have never called anybody a pig in this house, the fact remains that you have done more mess than anyone in the house anyways!" "I thank God that you got us to do all the chores when we were young, you compelled us to do all dishes. Yes I can do it all but now I am too busy to handle most of these chores all because of what you got me into. Yes I no longer regret having the children, you on your own promised to take care of them and that is why you are here to help." Grandma Pedro was very offended, her response was. "Yes I voluntarily decided to help, I have now voluntarily decided to leave." She stormed into her room to pack her belongings. She stood in shock, while her mother packed her belongings in the house. Her mother-in-law watched the unpleasant awkward development. She regretted coming to stay with them. She decided to mediate between her daughter-in-law and her mother to no avail. Angelina was sober, she went to her mother to plead that she should not leave the house in rage. She was pushed off and scolded as a stupid child that thought she knew better than her mother. On this note Grandma

Briggs waded into the issue. She pled that Grandma Pedro should wait for Zach to return before she left. "Wait for who? So that he should add his insult to my injury, are you not all in same camp? Didn't I tell you in the past that I knew you're scheming against my presence in the house of your son? Please do not come into this issue with your hypocrisy." Grandma Briggs was mesmerized. She looked at Grandma Pedro in disdain and questioned, "Mam, why is it that you always pull me into your troubles? Have I ever had a confrontation with you on any issue?" Grandma Pedro yelled, "...green-snake under green-grass... please leave me alone and let me go away from the house of your son."

Angelina was shocked to see her husband when she turned in response to a sound behind her. It pained her badly that her husband heard the last statement of her mother. She couldn't control her tears, but her mother was indifferent to the presence of Zach, she cared less whether he heard her or not. Her only comment in connection with Zach was that, "It is good you are here, your wife will tell you the story of why I have to go back to my husband. You are her husband, please keep your wife with you. I do not need to see her around me ever". Angelina continued crying. She had many reasons to cry. Her husband could not resist the pains and agony of his wife. He joined her in the tear-flow but Grandma Pedro was indifferent. She moved out of the house, called a cab and waited outside for the cab to come. Suddenly there was a storm and she was drenched. She stood in the rain and refused to come back inside the house. The cab came and off she went back to join her husband. Angelina did her best to contact her father on phone to no avail. The system said his phone had been switched off. It was a very bad experience for them all.

The following day, Grandma Briggs notified her son that she would have to leave due to the very unfortunate development. Her son quickly informed her that his wife is really struggling with depression over the issue. He pleaded that she should not make such a move as it may make his wife become mentally broken. His mother assured him that she would do everything within her power to make his wife happy. Angelina refused to leave her bedroom. She felt her Mother-in-law must have been greatly offended by her mother and may blame her for all the negative developments. Zach pled with his mother to go into their bedroom to see his wife and try to encourage her. His mother declined the proposal of her going into their matrimonial room. However, she promised her son that she would go to the entrance of the room to call her out. She went to the entrance of the bedroom and called on her daughter-in-law. Angelina was thrilled by the gentle and sonorous voice of her mother-in-law. She got out of bed to meet with her, she embraced her mother-in-law and pleaded that she should forgive her and her mother for all that happened the previous day. Her apology was accepted with some words of assurance that the care of the children would be her priority. Her countenance brightened up as she embraced her mother-in-law. She kissed her cheeks left and right and assured her that she had the liberty to scold her whenever she was wrong. In her heart of heart she adopted her as her mother. Grandma Briggs cuddled her and said, "I assure you of my love. You have always been my daughter. Remember my promises when we met for the very first time that your husband introduced you to me. I assured you that if you turn out to be a true wife of my son, who you have proved to be, you will not have a mother-in-law but a second mother." With excitement Angelina jumped on her mother-in-law's neck shouting, "I remember, thank you Mommy, thank you Mommy." On this note her mother-in-law said, "... we have a task, it is how to reconcile you with your biological mother so that you will have us both." The countenance of Angelina dropped, she looked at her Mother-in-law and said, "Your wish is my command."

CHAPTER THREE

THE INANIMATE THIRD-PARTY

Whatever is lifeless is said to be inanimate. Such is not in the manner of animal or human. Though plants have life but they are many times referred to as inanimate because they do not possess the ability to make decisions or respond intelligently to issues. There is however the tendency for an individual to fall in love or be obsessed with an inanimate. The life story of Matthew and Justina is a typical example of obsession with the inanimate.

Matthew was a lanky and handsome looking young man. His physique was a major force of attraction that endeared him to Justina. Their courtship was brief and the relationship was consummated in few months. They had everything working in their favor. Matthew had bought a two bedroom house few years before their wedding. He had planted some shrubs and trees and bonded with his plants. The house was conspicuous in the neighborhood due to the well nurtured organized shrubs and regularly replaced seasonal flowering plants. They were fond of each other and had mutual respect for their animate and inanimate pets respectively. Justina was in love with her dog, an animal that Matthew had to create interest in.

Their union was blessed with a baby boy in the first year of their marriage. Justina suggested that they buy a bigger house but Matthew was not ready to part with his plants that were his pride in the neighborhood. The argument and agitations ensued but climaxed when they had their second child, a baby girl. It was obvious that they needed a bigger house but as at that time, Matthew's shrubs were fully grown and more attractive. Instead of consenting to his wife's proposal to buy preferably a brand new house that will be built to their taste. He expressed the idea that they extend the present house with three additional rooms. His application for the extension was declined by the housing association in control of the neighborhood. He was disappointed and could not share the response of the housing association with his wife. He kept the letter away from her. His wife waited endlessly. When she could bear it no more, she approached the housing association on her own only to learn that their application for the extension was declined over six months ago. She was enraged and determined to vent her pains on her husband. It was not a pleasant discussion as Justina insisted that they move out of the house for a bigger accommodation. It was obvious that Matthew was not ready to part with his more cherished plants. His wife accused him of having more affection for the plants than his family. Though he could not deny the obvious but yet refused to address the reality. His claim was that his income and credit score could not afford the size and quality of the house he would want to buy. In his opinion, they were to manage the present home until they are more financially buoyant.

Few weeks later, Justina came home with a note of approval from the bank for a loan that would comfortably afford the family a purchase of the home of their choice. The news was received with no excitement by her husband. He was enraged and accused his wife of highhandedness. She was not responsive to any of his tantrums. She only pleaded with him. At a point she promised to pay for the transplantation of his major plants. His countenance became radiant. He agreed to his wife's plan for a relocation. Justina approached the horticultural corporation on the proposed transplantation of their palm trees and citrus plants. It was to cost them over five thousand Dollars. The note has it that the plants may not be transplanted in the fall but in the spring so as to grant a good growth condition to survive the transplantation shock. It implied they had additional six months to wait. The survival of the palm trees were guaranteed but not the citrus plants. At this juncture, Matthew agreed to break ties with his plants. Justina had stooped to conquer. Everything worked in their favor. They got the house of their choice in one of the best new layouts in a very good neighborhood. They moved in with excitement and mixed feelings over the issue of their furniture, Matthew was of the opinion that they get a new set of furniture for the new home but Justina wanted them to keep the furniture she bought when she moved in to join her husband after their wedding few years back. She claimed the proposal of her husband for new furniture was not of any economic advantage especially because the furniture was not looking bad for the new home. The fact was that she had a form of sentimental bond with the furniture. She did everything possible to make her husband find it difficult to change the furniture. She demanded for things that she knew her husband could not afford and if he could afford them, it will make the purchase of any new furniture unaffordable. Her husband had knowledge of her game but could not beat her demands. Matthew was bent on retaliation. He demanded that his wife cut off her long fingernails. His reason was that the nails were responsible for

Justina inability to handle some of the chores for which they paid a maid company. The argument lingered for months. His wife was not going to let go of the nails she had nurtured for a good number of years. She told her husband that the nails were her pets and were like children to her. She claimed she had had them before marrying him. The assertions made no sense to her husband. He insisted that the nails should be cut but Justina would not consent. On many occasions he called his wife disobedient and recalcitrant. Justina found the statement to be demeaning and derogatory. Their relationship was strained but they managed to keep things going.

The frontage of the new house was left bare but for a miserable looking half dead tree and uninviting baby-shrubs that were tucked into the ground by the builder company. Matthew looked at them with a great disdain, he determined to make the new property the envy of the neighbors in the next few months. Justina was very proud of her accomplishment. She arrived home in company of her friends to have a walk-through of the new home. They met Matthew in the front of the house trying to put one or two things right. She proudly introduced her husband to her friends. She told them to look at the frontage of the house very well so that they would appreciate the changes that her husband would affect soonest. She turned to one of her friends and said, "Please take the picture and let the number on the wall show because you may not recognize this house when next you come." With a smile the friend took a snapshot of the building. They all smiled as she added, "I am proud I married a man who has a good taste when it comes to what his environment looks like." One of her friends smilingly chipped in, "And what his wife looks like... I guess you have been his wise investment". "Except for my finger nails," Justina mused. Matthew felt he was well presented, with a smile he said, "My investment is very good, attractive and very pleasurable but for the finger nails that unstructured her productivity." Justina walked away briskly as her friends looked at each other's face. It was a good get-together but Justina did not like the closing statement of her husband.

Tammy was almost six years old, his father was bent on getting him to work along with him on most of the house chores, especially on the horticulture and minor farming at the back of the house. The Idea was not pleasing to his mother. She felt the young lad was too young for such exposure to strains. His father was bent on engaging him in whatever he did around the house. His belief was that '...an undomesticated child would grow to become a liability to his or her spouse in marriage'. In one of their arguments on the issue, he was close to convincing his wife, but she would not desist from indulging her children. On one sunny day, Matthew engaged his boy on farming at the back of the house. Little Tammy asked his father, "Dad, why are we planting these vegetables and tomatoes...can't we just buy them from the market? We are working too haaarrrd! This looks like slavery." His father was shocked, he could not imagine the little boy would make reference to slavery. He turned to him and questioned, "What do you know about slavery?" "Slaves were meant to do hard work," Tammy retorted. In his imagination, he believed it was 'his mother's voice'. He did his best to convince his son that men ought to be toughened by experience. The boy nodded his head conscientiously. However he was only in obedience to his father's desire. He preferred the indulgence granted by his mother.

Matthew had always been a very conservative person, his approach to usage and maintenance of personal items was very much at variance with that of his wife. He was trying to fix one of his "trainers" that he had had for more than three years in active use. His wife was angry watching him spend time attempting to put the shoes back into use. She assured him that she was going to dispose of the aging trainers that had evidently seen good days. He warned her never to try throwing his property into the garbage. Few weeks later, she came home with two brand new pairs of trainers in attempt to replace the old one. Her gift was appreciated but the old trainers were not disposed of. A month later, she took the old trainers out of sight with a claim that they have been thrown into the garbage. Very hot argument ensued. It was very bad. At a point Matthew said, "My trainers have not caused as much ugliness in this house as much as your dog and nurtured fingernails did." Justina was very offended. Her interpretation of the statement was that she was a domestic liability in the house. She insulted the intelligence of her husband when she said, "I thought I was dealing with a modern and civilized man that would know when an object or substance has outlived its value." Her husband was very enraged. He walked up to her, held her wrist firmly and sternly warned her never to address him the way she just did. Justina never saw her husband in such a ferocious anger. She was scared, the fear was obvious on her face. The grip was best compared to the strength of a blacksmith's vise. Leaving her, he said, "You either get rid of those nails or you bring my trainers back." In his imagination, the trainers must have been taken away by the dust men that took away the trash bags in the bin. He was surprised when his wife strolled in from the back of the house and threw his old trainers at him. He looked at her confused. He said, "Those nails are the cause of contention in this home. If you want your peace, you better get rid of them and function in your full capacity as a woman in this home. If you don't do it, I will do it myself. His wife fleered up and said, "If you try it, you would have blown it. Please don't dare me, you are already gradually making me hate you." Though shocked by his wife's threat, he felt she was only being defiant. He picked up his old pairs of trainers and walked away to the garage to put them back where they were normally at.

There was cold war which was evident to the children and the pets. Matthew never gave his wife's dog any treat. His wife refused to water any of the indoor plants nor border herself with the survival of the ones in the very hostile sun of the summer. Matthew did not have a clear understanding of the statement of his wife, "If you try it, you would have blown it." In his wildest imagination, he could not imagine the possible consequence of his intended action if he forcefully cut the fingernails of his wife. He woke his wife up from sleep and said, "Would you allow your nails to divide us?" His wife replied, "I guess my nails are more decent than your old trainers". Matthew was silent but determined to cut the nails when his wife was asleep. He got a nail cutter and was set to do the unexpected. He had a premonition of prospective interpretation of his intended action but he was not sensitive enough to listen to the whisper of the spirit. He had just clipped one of the fingernails when his wife woke up. She opened her eyes. She fought back like a wounded tiger. It was their first fight. She slapped her husband and accused him of dangerous act. She claimed she no longer felt safe in the house, that her husband could kill her in her sleep if he could cut her fingernail while she was asleep. The circumstance went out of hand. Matthew could not imagine the cause for the level of her reaction. Her interpretation of his action was too serious and outrageous for his thinking. He pleaded to no avail to her understanding. Though he had a black-eye but could not call the police. He wanted peace at all cost but his wife was just too sadistic.

Matthew called on their pastor to intervene in the matter. The pastor pleaded to no avail. Justina claimed she was no longer safe in the house. It was a good time for the pastor to come around. The front doorbell rang and the pastor was let in. Justina was still fuming with anger while her husband was still struggling to understand the implication of his action. The pastor pleaded for forgiveness. Justina claimed to have forgiven her husband but was just concerned about her safety. She went on to say, "Sir, with all due respect, would you feel safe and secured with a spouse that did what my husband came up with? The pastor responded, "My life is hid with Christ in God. I am the apple of God's eye.... making reference to the scriptures, Col. 3: 3 and Zech. 2: 8. Justina was silent. She suddenly erupted, "Sir, you have not answered my question. You are not being real. Would you have asked your daughter to feel safe with such a man that would do what my husband just did?" The pastor did not feel comfortable with her question and approach. He however determined to bury his pride and try to solve the problem on ground. He humorously responded, "I have always addressed you as my daughter and would treat you as one. The truth is, safety belongs to God. What your husband did was no doubt outrageous and demeaning. I guess it was a display of cowardice not an intent to destroy the love, trust and confidence that existed in your relationship." "He did that already," Justina interrupted. The pastor continued "...You will need to forgive him and do not allow the devil to blow this experience out of reasonable proportion." "But pastor, would you believe he that can cut the nails can cut the throat?" She questioned. The pastor took a deep breath. With a sigh he said, "Brethren, the devil is at work. He must have built on your unspoken differences to cause this to happen." Looking Matthew straight in the eyes, he said, "How I wish you were bold enough to resolve your differences on the issue of her fingernails and not go about it cowardly." Matthew was about to talk but was cautioned by the Spirit not to interrupt the pastor. The pastor continued, "My daughter, has he ever raised his hands against you?" "Not really, he once almost cracked my wrist when I insulted him. If he were to be a little child or someone I could apprehend when he did what he did, I would have been able to do what exactly I wanted to do. But he is my husband, I was only able to insult him. Yes I insulted him, his grip told me more about him than he thought. I do not know what I would do that will make him strangulate me in my sleep. It may be an expression of his cowardice"

Matthew was getting agitated and felt insulted that his action was born out of cowardice. He raised his right hand to suggest that the pastor should grant him the permission to talk. The pastor declined his request. The compulsory silence imposed on him by the pastor built up an emotional outburst in him. There came a sudden wailing from Matthew. He wept like a baby. His sudden breakdown was very over whelming to the pastor than to his wife. Initially she felt vindicated. And happy that she got him broken.

She had never seen her husband cry neither had she seen him do anything outrageous. She knew some thing unusual must have happened. She remembered some of the teachings in her psychology class that extremity may lead to negative or positive un-expected action or reaction. She felt a further push on her husband may incur a negative result. She was anxious to hear her husband speak. She turned to the pastor and request that her husband should be allowed to talk. The request was granted. Matthew subbed as he muttered, "How I wish Jesus would come right now to take me home. I have always loved my wife and children. I have to fend for and defend them. How I wish I knew how to handle this matter better than I did. The Bible says a good name is rather to be chosen. I do not wish to live with the tag of a potential murderer. Yes what I did was mean and stupid but the implication, interpretation and consequences are too hard for me to bear... he subbed. His subbing destroyed the emotional defense walls of his wife. She joined him. It was a sober moment. The pastor cut in and said, "Would you at this moment forgive each other? Please remember the attributes of love as stated in the Bible, 1Cor. 13. They both agreed to forgive each other. Turning to the pastor Justina said, "Sir, I guess I need some time to get over the trauma, would you agree that I stay away for some few days. The pastor was a little hesitant. He was about to speak when Matthew said he would be ready to accept whatever his wife sees as a recipe for peace and restoration.

Ruminating over the whole developments, Matthew realized that the idea of him cutting his wife's fingernails when she was asleep was suggested by one of her friends that had insinuated some passes to him which he cleverly ignored. He thought of how mischievous and evil friend she was to his wife. He realized that his wife was actually in danger as long as their friendship continues. He knew that his wife would have shared the ongoing issue with her scenically destructive friend. There was no way he could successfully convince his wife that the idea was from one of her friends. He decided to find a way to paint a perfect picture of all that had happened. The idea was to have a recorded telephone conversation with his wife's obnoxious friend. He felt her behavior was a contradiction of her name; Justina. In a broad soliloquy he said, "Justice must be done. She has not been fair at all..." It was the counsel of Juliana that Justina should stay away from her husband for a while. Her ploy was to actually gain access to Matthew. In her counsel, she advised her friend to go to the house of the third in their team, Paulin. Justina notified her parents of the state of her marriage. Her father consented to the idea of her moving out for a while but her mother shared a contrary opinion. She said, "I know quite well that you are already traumatized and tormented by the spirit of fear. I want to assure you that your life is hidden in Christ with God." She intuitively added, "Personally I am not comfortable with your team of friends. They may be instrumental to the breakdown of your marriage especially because they are divorced." She refuted her mother's insinuation. However she was unable to dismiss it off her mind.

It was almost a week that Justina had moved out of her matrimonial home. Matthew called her friend Juliana soliciting her plea to his wife. He was shocked when Justina said her friend had overreacted on the issue of his attempt to clip off her finger nails. She went on, "Why should she move out of her home, who does she expect to take care of the children. Did she make arrangements for your feeding before she abandoned you? At least I cautioned her that if she must move to Paulin's house, she must go with the children and store enough food in the freezers for you to take care of yourself. Were these arrangements put in place?" Matthew was quiet. "Are you there?" She questioned. "Yes my dear." Matthew absent mindedly responded. "Is she there with you?" Matthew realized his error and tendered an apology. You don't have to, we are all dear to each other. I am sure you already missed her. You cannot get her back right now. She needs to sleep over her imaginations. Feel free to check on her at Pauline's place. I guess she will allow you to have a dinner on your visit. I am quite very busy right now, I would have offered to prepare you a dinner." She concluded. Matthew felt the recording was not strong enough to indict her. He said, "If I knew she was going to react this bad to clipping off her fingernail while asleep as you suggested, I would not have tried it." "Forget about all these nonsense. What is the big deal about her fingernails. If she must wear nails why not occasional. She could do that with the artificial. I don't even like the idea that she wore natural nails. I actually thought she would take it lightly but she has obviously overreacted. I guess she had wanted to find an excuse for divorce, a path she already set on by this separation," she asserted. Matthew excused himself and the conversation was ended. He sat and listened to the recorded conversation. He was satisfied.

It was a Friday, Justina missed her home and her children. She never picked the repeated phone calls of her husband. She felt lonely and would want to see her children if not her husband. She decided to arrive their school early at the closing time so as to pick them before her husband would do so. The traffic was not to her advantage, her husband had already picked the children before she got to the school. She watched her husband drive out of the school with her children strapped at the backseat. She decided to trail his movement. He did not drive too far before he stopped at a fast food restaurant. As he parked his car, his wife pulled up into the next parking bay. He was excited to see his wife. His exuberance was very surprising to Justina who was ready for a showdown. He rushed forward to embrace his wife as the children struggled trying to get out of the seatbelts. She felt weary and sad. She could not hide her emotions as she never expected such acceptance. She could not resist the curdle of her husband. The children jumped on her with multiple questions. She sobbed. Her husband held her closely as he said, "This is a moment of truth. Please be kind enough to listen to me telling you the truth." She was eager to listen. Matthew brought out his phone. Played the recorded conversation between him and her friend Juliana. She could not believe her ears. She repeatedly requested her husband to rewind the recording before the entire tape was done with. She burst into tears, she sobbed as she tore off her fingernails with her teeth. Her husband was shocked but excited. She blamed herself for her mistrust and misplaced confidence.

The Holy Spirit expounded the previous comment of her mother. She cried aloud and called the attention of some bystanders. She suddenly realized that they were in a public place. To save her face in case the people misconceive the development and call the police, she embraced her husband and gave him a very electrifying kiss. Their son Tammy clapped his hands in approval. It was his first time of seeing his parents in such heartfelt romance in a public place. She pleaded with her husband to let her drive to their home with the children in her car. She was obligated. It was time for lunch. The children were very hungry as their parents forgot the reason why they stopped at the fast food restaurant. Justina went straight into her kitchen and in no time made a sumptuous lunch for them all. It was a moment of truth and reunion. The children enjoyed themselves and were assisted on their homework. Justina was doing all the talking as they walked hand in hand into their bedroom. Her husband held her close to himself and gave her a wonderful kiss all over. He held her hands and kissed the fingers she had "beheaded". It was a very exhilarating moment for them both. She looked at her husband in the eyes with tears rolling down her cheeks as she said, "I cannot imagine the devil building on my obsession to destroy my home. Yes, I heard all the evil intentions of Juliana but I decided to heed her advice that if at all I will wear nails, they will be artificial at my desired occasion." With a perfect expression of love her husband pulled her closer and poured the fullness of his heart to her. It was a perfect reconciliation.

There was no doubt that they both learnt to be careful and sensitive to realize the danger, when the inanimate or any pet becomes a source of obsession, obstruction or bone of contention in their marriage or other relationships. They realized, *"Danger could not be more dangerous than the ignorance of its existence"*

CHAPTER FOUR

THE SUPERNATURAL [INVISIBLE] THIRD-PARTY

The realm of the spirit is very deep and beyond any human control or comprehension. There is no doubt that the spiritual realm rules the physical. The supernatural realm has two parts to it. The negative [demonic] and the positive [divine]. This is the realm from which impersonating, obsessive, oppressive and possessive spirits emanate to take control of the physical being of their victims. An individual operating under the influence of negative supernatural forces may or may not be aware of the very force or forces working in his/her life. Such forces are responsible for the experience of the individual in any relationship or dealings.

An individual may be aware of a being or supernatural identifiable force that appears in his/her sleep. The individual may be very much aware that he or she has a tie with a particular force or is controlled by a particular force. This force is either a spirit-husband or spirit-wife. In some cases, the force may just always appear as a helper. The person assisted by this negative supernatural force may be pleased with the assistance given by the force or forces especially at crucial and challenging moments. Such individual may enjoy the assistance of the forces. The force or forces may be in control of the life experience and relationship of the said individual. In most cases it is always beyond the control of the affected person until the individual is delivered by the power in the blood of Jesus Christ. The invisible third party may cause a lot of conflicts and horrible things in a relationship. The spouse of a person who has a marriage agreement with an invisible third party may always experience misfortunes as a result of the attacks of the jealous spiritual spouse. Every genuine Christian is ruled and controlled by the Holy Spirit.

The fact remains that a spirit filled child of God cannot be demon possessed but can be demon obsessed or oppressed due to spiritual carelessness or laziness. This is the reason why anyone that decides to follow Jesus must be spiritually vibrant. Many Christians are spiritually empty but very actively involved in religious rites and rituals. Their activities may favor the church but infuriate the devil who builds on their spiritual emptiness to victimize them. In most cases people always have to question why bad things happen to good people. The major weapons of a good Christian are holiness, watchfulness at the place of prayer and adequate knowledge of the word of God. It is very unfortunate that many Christians do not realize that their failures to pay these "insurance premiums" are responsible for their misfortunes or predicaments.

Some of the narratives below are adapted from true life stories.

WHERE IS BONIFACE?

Boniface was attracted to a beautiful lady called Rose. The wedding was a colorful one that attracted friends and foes from various parts of the community. After the first three years into the marriage the couple realized that something was wrong as it obviously became impossible for them to have children after all their efforts were to no avail. They were invited to a Christian meeting where they eventually gave their lives to Jesus. They were given assurance by the brethren that with God nothing shall be impossible. They sought for spiritual assistance because of the experience of Rose in her dreams. The pastor showed a great concern but had no clue on what to do.

A lady evangelist was invited to the church for a weekend ministration service. The presence of God was very tangible at the meeting. A ministration session ensued and Sister Rose was the focal point. Her manifestation was suggestive of a movement that was not clearly understood by the ministers. When she regained her consciousness she was asked about where she went while wriggling on the floor and throwing her hands into the air. She was shocked and thought everyone saw all that she did or heard all the conversations that took place in the realm of the spirit. She claimed to have gone into the Marine world where she was given a wonderful welcome by her spiritual-husband and children. The whole scene was like a trance to her husband. The minister turned to her and asked whether she was ready to renounce and disown the spiritual husband and children. After a brief silence she said, "I love 'my Bonny' but I am not ready to let go of my family in the Marine world." It was a very scary experience for her physical husband. Few months later he ran away and no one was able to track him. Everybody was asking, "Where is Boniface?"

The invisible third-party ruined their marriage.

GEISHA THE BEAUTY QUEEN

The Bible says, *"Favour is deceitful, and beauty is vain: but a woman that feareth the Lord, she shall be praised."* Proverbs 31:30 KJV

The Amplified bible makes it very animating, *"Charm and grace are deceptive, and [superficial] beauty is vain, But a woman who fears the LORD [reverently worshiping, obeying, serving, and trusting Him with awe-filled respect], she shall be praised."* Proverbs 31:30 AMP

Briscoe was a very successful brother in the church that had membership of about a thousand, fifty percent of which were young ladies most of them professionals. Geisha was a very charming beautiful lady that very few men could walk past and not give a second glance. She once caused a brother to run into another woman with a bowl of soup during a get-together in the church. Most men called her "Too-much." They were obviously intimidated. Not many thought of dating her or that they were able to match her strong leadership qualities as displayed in her personal business and the church as a whole. To Briscoe, she was just a sister whom he believed would boost his ego if it happened that they got married. He was not too handsome looking but a financial pillar in the church.

Geisha had had interest in Briscoe, but could not vent her feelings. With her expectation, there was no much resistance but the usual feminine reluctance when Briscoe expressed his interest. The pastor was informed and the marriage was contracted in no time especially because they both were long matured for marriage in both material and age. The wedding was almost put off when Briscoe informed his parents that since his engagement to Geisha he always had conflicts in his dreams with a man that he could almost find on the street. He claimed many times he walked the street looking for this invisible man as he perceived he was always around him.

The wedding was conducted on the persuasion of the Pastor's words of assurance, "...*Greater is He that is in you than he that is in the world.*" 1John 4: 4.

It was a celebration session for the newly wedded when Geisha took in the very first month of their marriage. Everything was fine but for the fact that the invisible spiritual spouse occasionally showed up in the bedroom especially when they were having sexual relationship. This in most cases had made him lost his turgidity or cause premature ejaculation. His wife would ask, "Darling, what happened." He would look blank, gazing in the direction where he saw the invisible third-party. He remembered he saw someone that looked like the said invisible man at their wedding reception. He could not express his dilemma to anyone. He determined to fast and do some spiritual warfare on the issue. When it seemed that he was only engaged in exercise in futility, he decided to go back to his pastor who had encouraged him that God is greater than any invisible force. He narrated his personal efforts, the pastor encouraged him that he was on the right line of action. They prayed together. It got to a head when Geisha suffered a miscarriage at four months of pregnancy. It all happened when she screamed from her sleep holding her tummy shouting, "Leave my baby, leave my baby." Briscoe opened his eyes and saw the spectral man running through the door with the baby in his hand. He held his wife as he shouted, "...it is the man, it is the invisible man, and see him.... ha ha." Shortly thereafter, Geisha started bleeding and it was the loss of the pregnancy. Briscoe was very angry and sad. The sorrow was overwhelming. He rushed out of the room as if to chase the invisible man. He knew that the issue at hand was spiritual but he could not but call the emergency services to rush his wife to the hospital. She was given the utmost care and attention but all to no avail. The pregnancy was lost. The fetus, the expected baby was given to them and they were expected to get a funeral undertaker for the burial. Briscoe took the picture of the fetus and informed the hospital that they would not want to go home with the fetus. It generated a lot of controversy however their opinion was respected because the chaplain said, 'taking the baby with them may traumatize them the more especially as they do not want to go home with it.' It was a baby boy.

The pastor came to the hospital to express his empathy and condolence. Holding Briscoe to himself he held Geisha's hand with his other hand as he prayed. After the prayers he said to the couple, "... the battle line is drawn. We shall fight this battle until we are victorious. Please do not fail to show up at the deliverance services held in the church every Monday. Before this time Briscoe and his wife had always believed that the deliverance sessions were for those who have demons or fighting the enemies that pursued them from their distant relatives who do not want them to succeed in life. The pastor tried to educate them on the subject of deliverance. He said, "If I have my way, I will compel every member of the church to come for the deliverance services. Deliverance is for all Christians. You never can tell when a demon is sent after you or when an old covenant was being reconnected. Deliverance is a necessity for a lasting peace in the Christian race." The couple looked at each other. Geisha said, "Pastor, I believe I need the deliverance. I have heard my husband talk of him seeing one "invisible man." He claimed he always saw the man in a flash and he disappeared. I am sure it must be the same man that I always see in my dream long before we got married. He always makes love with me in my dreams. I felt sexually fulfilled. That was partly the reason why I was not eager to get married." Briscoe realized that he was fully engrossed with similar experience in his bachelorhood. He did not vent his experience. He believed that it was infatuation or imaginary sex with ladies that led to his wet dreams.

The pastor informed his wife who happened to be a co-minister in the church about the big blow that hit the church, the brethren in particular. She wept bitterly for the loss of the pregnancy of Sis Geisha. They have been close friends because she was involved with her in the children ministry of the church. The pastor said, "I have mandated them to show up for deliverance as soon as she leaves the hospital." "My dear, you'll remember I told you that this couple needed to come for deliverance before they got married. They need to destroy all the hands of the enemies from their respective fathers or mothers houses. Any enemy of the family must die..." The pastor interrupted her, "I guess it is not the enemies from their fathers or mothers houses but spiritual husband and spiritual wife on both sides I believe." "Whichever enemy from the pit of hell, they must all die." The pastor's wife insisted. The pastor humorously said, "From anywhere, they must all die..." His wife said, "I don't care whether you believe, or agree or disagree that there are enemies from their fathers or mothers house or not, every force, man, woman, demon, principality or power must die." With a little tincture of laughter he added, "My Dear, demons or spirits do not die, we can only cast them out." "Die or cast, they must just leave these brethren alone." "Only the brethren?" He questioned. "My dear, leave me alone, let them die" she retorted. Her husband with laughter said "Am I the demon, you said I should leave you alone." "Ok, you are not the demon but don't allow the demons to live around us. Every enemy must die."

The deliverance was scheduled. Praise and worship was going on when Briscoe fell and was manifesting having sex with an invisible partner. The pastor quickly set in and rebuked the foul spirit. He commanded the spirit of fornication and adultery to get out and go into the pit of hell. The spirit was about to speak through him but the pastor shut him up and commanded the spirit never to return. There were lots of agitations and almost a violent aggression when the pastor shouted, "...go, go, go, goooooooo." Suddenly the aggression subsided and Briscoe opened his eyes and jumped up trying to run in the direction of the door. He was held back by the pastor and the brethren. When he was asked about what happened, he said, "I want to follow her." The pastor laid his hands on him and said, "I separate you from her in the mighty name of Jesus Christ." Briscoe fell to the ground and stretched as if he had an epileptic feat. His wife was scared to the skin of her teeth. She screamed, "Don't let him die...." the pastor, though also scared, shouted, "Get out completely and never return..." Briscoe was calm and he opened his eyes. The pastor questioned him about what was going on. He said, "I saw Jazzy going out of me and I pursued her. I realized that some hands pulled me back and she came back into me with some of her friends. I fell and I heard the pastor command her to get out of me and never to come back. They all fled and I felt light," the pastor laid hands on him again and he was speaking in the Holy Ghost. He was left on the floor.

Geisha was scared when the pastor moved towards her. She moved back and the pastor's wife held her hands. She went violent and pushed the pastor's wife back. The pastor's wife said, "I come against you in the name of Jesus Christ. She roared like a lion and fell to the ground. Suddenly the voice of a man spoke, "You think you can get away from me? You are not going anywhere." "Who are you," The pastor's wife questioned. "I am her husband, she is my property. I made her beautiful and great. This idiot wants to take her from me...ha ha ha, you are wasting your time. She has my children. You cannot get her away from me," the spirit yelled. "What is your legal ground in her life?" Asked the pastor's wife. "Ask her, she knew that her mother asked for her from us. We cannot let her go. She is for me in the Marine world." One of the ministers that stood by shouted, "Come out of her. " The body of Geisha rose from the floor and gave the minister a very horrible slap. With a scream the voice said, "shut up you adulterer. I would have thought you a lesson if not that I have been partially disarmed since I came in here." As the pastor moved forward to rescue his minister, the demonic spirit said, "You better keep him away, before I finish him." The pastor's wife commanded the spirit to say what the minister did. The force responded, "Ask him, he will tell you the truth if he is not ready to die." The minister started crying as he walked out of the ministration. The pastor was very angry both with the minister and the demon that had wasted the life of a child. He commanded the spirit to come out but the spirit questioned him whether he was ready to face the consequence of his action. The pastor was shocked. He questioned impulsively, "What action? What consequence?" "You will have the ordinary Geisha." Responded the foul spirit. The pastor hated any lengthy dialogue with the devil. He commanded the evil force to go out in the mighty name of Jesus. Suddenly there was a change which was obvious about the body on the floor. It could not be explained by any human mind or logic. There seemed to be no physical difference in the appearance or look of the known Sister Geisha but it was obvious to all that something was missing. She was just not charming. The pastor was afraid. His wife was scared, Briscoe felt the person on the floor was not his wife. He could not feel the affection and love. He was in a different world. He felt the marriage was over with. The wife of the pastor shouted on the body before them, "HOLY-GHOST FIRE". FIRE, FIRE, FIRE...." It was like a movie as the body seemed to be burning and Geisha was responding as if to put off the burning fire. A passerby heard the call of fire repeatedly. He thought somebody was trapped in the fire within the building. He called 911. In few minutes, the fire fighters were in same hall with the brethren. The evil spirit raised the body of Geisha and said, "So, you have come to put off fire, when you see real fire, can you stand? Get out of here before I set you on fire" They stepped backward as the pastor informed them that there was no physical fire but Holy Ghost fire. One of them happened to be a Christian. He had the under standing and watched his colleagues mesmerized by the demon. They walked out and drove off. The pastor and his wife knew that Geisha was not yet completely freed. The pastor's wife said to the spirit, "I know you are still there, I command you, take every property of yours in the life of Sister Geisha and go to the pit of hell. She fell and started screaming "bill, nooooo." The pastor said, "It is a command. Go to the lake of fire in the mighty name of Jesus Christ." There was sudden silence. She opened her eyes and asked, "What is happening? The pastor's wife responded with a smile and congratulated her. She looked at herself and burst into tears. As she was crying the pastor was prompted to sing a popular song,

"Let the glory of the Lord come down 2ce,

Let the glory of the Lord from heaven come down,

Let the glory of the Lord come down."

The whole atmosphere changed. As Geisha sang with them, she started smiling. In few minutes her husband rushed her and carried her off the ground. The pastor was surprised. When questioned, her husband said, "I just loved her, I cannot say why. It was a night of great deliverance. They were about to leave the hall when the minister that was convicted of sin by both the devil and the Holy Spirit stepped in. He confessed his evils practices and asked for the brethren to forgive and pray for him. The pastor was still thinking of necessary disciplinary actions and sanctions against him. The pastor's wife laid hands on him and another deliverance session started. Every foul spirit in him was cast out. He went home rejoicing.

The pastor had to explain to the couples to see each other as clean children of God. He was prompted to play the recording of the session for Briscoe so that he may clearly see that it was not only his wife that was delivered. He was surprised. He asked series of questions to which the pastor gave very satisfactory answers. They both were happy and freed. Briscoe and his wife were later blessed with a set of twins, Faith and Faithful. They never suffered any more in the hands of invisible spouse. Briscoe addressed his wife as, "My Queen."

CHAPTER FIVE

THE CONCEALED THIRD PARTY

Whatsoever is said to be concealed is hidden from human sight, though the impact of its existence cannot be denied or reasonably ignored. The concealed third party could function at various levels. It could always build on human, animal or nature to manifest its evils. It may be very difficult to place the source of the consequential experience. Every human action is in response to a superior force that has the capability of ruling the mind. There is no doubt that man may sell himself or herself to a force through involvements or lines of action or reaction. Sexual relationship is a blood covenant. Diseases or spiritual forces can be transmitted through contacts such as kisses, oral sex, conventional sex even a shake of hands. A concealed third party may cause a spouse to act or react contrary to expectation.

Jessy lost her mother at the brink of their wedding date. She was the only child of her mother. She never had any close relationship with her father or any of his relatives. In her wildest imagination, her husband was going to be her confidant. She survived the shock due to the supports from the brethren and the church.

Teddy was very sexually wayward before he came into marriage with his lovely wife Jessy. He had jilted many ladies who had determined to deal with him on the issues of marriage or fortune in life. He had no idea of the spiritual personality of any of the ladies he had jilted. His marriage vow was violated on many instances. His wife was suspicious of his infidelity but she chose to conceal it from her parents or in-laws. She was bent on making her marriage work. She tried her best to satisfy her husband, but to no avail. Teddy was a very easy going handsome young man that reposed confidence in seeking comfort and ease at little or no strain to his cherished lifestyle. His disposition was best described as a frozen sea. His illicit relationships were in complete betrayal of his composure and temperamental traits. He was believed to be a phlegmatic melancholic. His wife had the notion that other ladies could be after her husband. She chose to indulge him beyond reasonable level. He took advantage of the situation to make demands on her. In most cases, his wish was her command. She was the breadwinner of the family. Though she had a medical condition that would naturally have prevented her from becoming pregnant. The Lord beheld her faithfulness and gave her a miracle son. The new addition to the family was named Issy.

Some concealed forces were in control of Teddy's life, he could not keep his eyes off other women or anything in skirt. He became addicted to websites that promoted Pornography. His marital relationship was strained more especially as there was nothing to write home about his Christian profession of faith. His wife felt tired of all the going on. She decided to lock him out of their home. She claimed he was not of any advantage but a source of pain and frustrations. He was a domestic liability. There was no doubt that his illicit relationships had drained him of the energy that could have afforded his wife any sexual satisfaction. His personal belongings were put into disposable bags and kept outside of the house. He felt humiliated and had to seek accommodation with his Aunt who had always played the role of mother in his life. His aunt and her husband had been his surviving parents. They decided to house him and keep watch over his moral life. It was not an easy task trying to keep track of a grown up adult. He had liberty to go to places of his choice. His "parents" believed, his stay under their roof would afford them the opportunity to impact his life and impress upon him the standard word of God. The Bible says,

"So faith comes from hearing [what is told], and what is heard comes by the [preaching of the] message concerning Christ." ROMANS 10:17 AMP

It was the practice of the family to come together in the morning for prayers. He got the laying on of hands almost every morning. His spiritual life was believed to have improved. He visited the residence of his wife. A conditional agreement was reached on their reunion. Arrangements were made on their reconciliation. Everything was almost working out fine. Suddenly, his wife declined all proposals about their reconciliation. Everyone was surprised by the sudden turn in plan. At this juncture it was obvious that there were concealed forces that made the reconciliation impossible.

The pastor invited Teddy to a meeting. He tried to make him realize that the battle at hand was beyond ordinary. He asked him to recall his past and the generational record of the family of his wife. He established the fact that they both had a battle to fight against concealed invisible third party. In his assertions, he said he strongly believed that any known platonic friend of his wife was planted by concealed forces to destabilize his home. He explained to him that he had great battles to fight. The battle was on how to break the generational trend of single parenthood in the lineage of his wife. The pastor did not mince words to tell him that he was under the sledge hammer of the curses or spells cast on him by the ladies he had jilted in the past.

He interrupted the pastor by saying, "...but the Bible says,

"Therefore if anyone is in Christ [that is, grafted in, joined to Him by faith in Him as Savior], he is a new creature [reborn and renewed by the Holy Spirit]; the old things [the previous moral and spiritual condition] have passed away. Behold, new things have come [because spiritual awakening brings a new life]."
2 CORINTHIANS 5:17 AMP

The pastor was quick to cut in, "...yes it was true you claimed to have given your life to Jesus. You lived with a lady in illicit relationship while you were undergoing all the stipulated procedures by the church for all potential candidates for ordination. Did you realize that that was wrong? You have not lived as someone who was convicted of sin but captivated by religious rites and rituals. You need to know the true meaning of Christianity. To be a Christian is to be Christ-like. Remember Apostle Paul's statement in his letter to the brethren in Rome:

"*Now the mind of the flesh is death [both now and forever--because it pursues sin]; but the mind of the Spirit is life and peace [the spiritual well-being that comes from walking with God--both now and forever]; the mind of the flesh [with its sinful pursuits] is actively hostile to God. It does not submit itself to God's law, since it cannot, and those who are in the flesh [living a life that caters to sinful appetites and impulses] cannot please God. However, you are not [living] in the flesh [controlled by the sinful nature] but in the Spirit, if in fact the Spirit of God lives in you [directing and guiding you]. But if anyone does not have the Spirit of Christ, he does not belong to Him [and is not a child of God]." ROMANS 8:6-9 AMP.*

Teddy was offended, he stood up to walk away on the pastor. The pastor instructed him to sit down. He reluctantly obeyed. He knew the implication of any disobedience or the magnitude of the insult if he disobeyed, as he was still living under the roof of the pastor. The pastor went on, "Realize you are not a stranger to me. In your own understanding, do you think it was right for you to serve as a sex-mate to a single parent who encouraged you to go to a bible college and do all the courses that will enable the church to ordain you? Remember the lady was then the leader of the evangelistic team of the church you attended? Do you believe she was a genuine child of

God? Was that not a curse. She must be a secret agent of the devil. There is no doubt she is likely to be a concealed third-party that has troubled your marital relationship." Teddy was quiet. The pastor perceived that he was offended. He said, "Do you have your bible with you? Please open it to Gal. 4: 16. He took out his phone and read:

"Where then is that gratulation of yourselves? For I bear you witness, that, if possible, ye would have plucked out your eyes and given them to me. So then am I become your enemy, by telling you the truth? They zealously seek you in no good way; nay, they desire to shut you out, that ye may seek them. But it is good to be zealously sought in a good matter at all times, and not only when I am present with you. My little children, of whom I am again in travail until Christ be formed in you—" Galatians 4:15-19 ASV

The pastor noticed that he started reading from verse 15. He did not correct him and did not stop him until he stopped on the nineteen verse. Looking straight into his eyes the pastor said, "You know I love you. If I do, I should not spare you." He took his bible and read: *"You have not yet struggled to the point of shedding blood in your striving against sin; and you have forgotten the divine word of encouragement which is addressed to you as sons, "MY SON, DO NOT MAKE LIGHT OF THE DISCIPLINE OF THE LORD, DO*

NOT LOSE HEART and GIVE UP WHEN YOU ARE CORRECTED BY HIM; F OR THE LORD DISCIPLINES and CORRECTS THOSE WHOM HE LOVES, AND HE PUNISHES EVERY SON WHOM HE RECEIVES and WELCOMES [TO HIS HEART]." You must submit to [correction for the purpose of] discipline; God is dealing with you as with sons; for what son is there whom his father does not discipline? Now if you are exempt from correction and without discipline, in which all [of God's children] share, then you are illegitimate children and not sons [at all]." HEBREWS 12:4-8 AMP

He went further to read from the old King James,

"But if ye be without chastisement, whereof all are partakers, then are ye bastards, and not sons." Hebrews 12:8 KJV

Teddy was convicted of sins. He wept bitterly and promised the pastor he was going to live right. The pastor took his phone and called Jessy to arrange a meeting in his attempt to reconcile her with her husband. The meeting was fixed to hold after one of the church regular programs. He tried frantically to convince Jessy to receive her husband back. He encouraged her to do her best to break every cycle of generational curses. The pastor was partially impressed that Jessy granted him attention and showed interest in the subject of the discussion. Jessy was on her way home, suddenly a force invaded her mind with the assurance of comfort without reconciling with her husband. She was overtaken by the concealed third-party. She told her husband that she was not ready for any reconciliation. The invisible concealed third-party painted a very ugly picture of her husband. Her friend Debbie who had suffered losing her husband to a strange woman due to similar lines of action cautioned her but to no avail. She remained a victim of invisible concealed third-party.

WHERE ARE YOU?

The question, "Where are you" could imply an expression of affection or suspicion.

The marital relationship of Jessica and Jack epitomized both.

It was love at first sight that eventually culminated into a marriage. Everything went on well until Jessica suspected that her husband was dating another woman. She could not establish her facts but was very uncomfortable with the movements of her husband. She could not trust him because it was impossible for her to live off the guilt of their courtship days. She could not forgive herself for their illicit sexual spree which they successfully concealed from their pastors and officiating ministers. She remembered her answer to the question of the minister who joined them together in a supposedly holy matrimony. The minister read from the church marriage order of service, "Does any of you have reason or reasons why you should not be joined together in holy matrimony?" To which they both answered, "No reason or reasons." She felt guilty that they both agreed to deceive the Lord. She remembered the regular statement of her pastor, "You will be daft to think, the person that agreed with you in attempt to deceive the Lord will not be able to deceive you." She felt hunted by her past sins, especially the abortion they procured. She remembered that her pastor had once said, "A lie is a monster, an invisible force that can ruin any relationship and destroy lives." She was obsessed by a force that turned her to a *"Monitoring gadget."* A force that attempted to rule the life of her husband. She remembered that the blood of Abel cried against Cain in the ears of God. She could not feel comfortable in her marriage. Many times she called on her husband to know his whereabout. She felt there were forces monitoring her much more than she could monitor her husband. The concealed forces were blood and lies. They were personified in her imagination and almost tangible as she regularly imagined the cry of the baby they aborted. In her guilt, the sins were believed to be responsible for her delayed experience of pregnancy.

Jack was not actually involved in any extra-marital sexual relationship but just got into a platonic relationship with a colleague at work. He was very conscious of his past and would not want to complicate his guilt. He had conditioned himself to the determination of Job: *"I made a covenant with my eyes not to look lustfully at a young woman. ²For what is our lot from God above, our heritage from the Almighty on high? ³Is it not ruin for the wicked, disaster for those who do wrong?"* (Job 31: 1-3) And the faithful-ness of Joseph: *"⁷ and after a while his master's wife took notice of Joseph and said, "Come to bed with me!" ⁸ But he refused. "With me in charge," he told her, "my master does not concern himself with anything in the house; everything he owns he has entrusted to my care. ⁹ No one is greater in this house than I am. My master has withheld nothing from me except you, because you are his wife. How then could I do such a wicked thing and sin against God?"* (Genesis 39: 7-9) His determination was gradually eroded as Jazmin wanted more than just a platonic relationship. He felt the only person he could report the circumstance to was his pastor. He believed that apart of his determination and promise to the Lord, he will not find it too easy to betray the confidence his pastor had reposed in him. Getting to his pastor, he was convicted of the sins of his past. He decided to confess his past sins especially his fornications, deceits and abortion. The pastor was shocked but impressed that he was convicted and therefore confessed. He prayed with him as he sobbed for his sins. The pastor seriously cautioned him on his platonic relationship with Jazmin. The pastor flipping through the pages of his bible, opened to 1 Thessalonians. 5: 22-23. He read,

"Abstain from every form of evil [withdraw and keep away from it]. Now may the God of peace Himself sanctify you through and through [that is, separate you from profane and vulgar things, make you pure and whole and undamaged--consecrated to Him--set apart for His purpose]; and may your spirit and soul and body be kept complete and [be found] blameless at the coming of our Lord Jesus Christ." 1 Thess. 5:22-23 AMP

He promised not to betray his marriage vow.

Jessica could not confess her sinful past. She was scared of the potential consequences, should the pastor take it out on her. ***Guilt is a force of servitude.*** She was awkward to her husband, her demeanor was questionable. She most of the time vented her guilt on her husband. She questioned his movements and monitored him with her phone. She had no idea that her husband had confessed to the pastor and thereby freed from guilt. She went through her notebook and read one of the catchphrases of her pastor. It read, *"Guilt is a killer monster that drains its victim of peace, joy and appreciable progress."* She pondered over it for a long while. Months later, she decided to confess her sins to the pastor. She adjudged her husband as being heartless and habitual adulterer. She spent more time trying to find faults in him but to no avail. She could not just understand how he was radiant and encouraging whenever she mentioned the issue of their delayed pregnancy. She again remembered that her pastor once said, *"Sin is a demon that torments and thrives on the adamancy of its victim through guilt."*

She decided to confess her sins. Her husband watched her mood but was surprised when she suddenly burst into laughter. He questioned, "What's funny?" "I just remembered the story pastor told about that little boy called Jerry. You remember?" "Was it the boy that accidentally killed the grandma's duck with a stone shot and buried it?" "O yes", she responded. "The grandma and his big sister saw him, but he felt his sin was not known to anyone. The big sister confronted him on the issue and eventually held him in bondage and servitude for months. He was compelled to do almost all the house chores. One day he was fed up of the torment and control by his sister. He decided and confessed his assumed hidden sin to his grandma. The grandma told him, "I saw you when you killed my duck, I was just watching to know for how long you would yield to the dictates and servitude of your sister..." Her husband quickly cut the story off with an excuse that he was about to catch up with a task on his job.

She felt he was not ready to face the pastor on the issue as she believed he knew where she was going on telling the story. Jack quickly called the pastor and pleaded with him that he should not let his wife know that he had confessed their sins to him. Same plea he made almost a year ago. She headed for the pastor's office. She sent a text to her husband indirectly and carefully telling him he should be ready to confess his sins. She made reference to Proverbs 28: 13,

"He who conceals his transgressions will not prosper, but whoever confesses and turns away from his sins will find compassion and mercy." PROVERBS 28:13 AMP

Her husband was very pleased that she was ready to tell the pastor about their dirty past. His only response was, "God is merciful." She concluded that her husband was insensitive to the possible implications of their past. She believed the contentions and confusions they had and all the fruitless efforts they have made on various aspects of life after their wedding may not be unconnected with the fact that the devil had been resident in their home. In a soliloquy she said, "I may not see the devil but I am convinced his hands are evident in our home." She met with the pastor, narrated the entire experience with tears especially as she felt the pastor had more confidence in her as a Sunday school teacher. The pastor pushed forward the box of tissue paper for her to wipe her tears and blow out her clogged but "drizzling" nostrils. He made reference to Proverbs 28: 13, James 4: 3-4, 8,

"You ask [God for something] and do not receive it, because you ask with wrong motives [out of selfishness or with an unrighteous agenda], so that [when you get what you want] you may spend it on your [hedonistic] desires. You adulteresses [disloyal sinners--flirting with the world and breaking your vow to God]! Do you not know that being the world's friend [that, loves the things of the world] is being God's enemy? So whoever chooses to be a friend of the world makes himself an enemy of God. Come close to God [with a contrite heart] and He will come close to you. Wash your hands, you sinners; and purify your [unfaithful] hearts, you double-minded [people]." JAMES 4:3-4, 8 AMP,

"Is anyone among you sick? He must call for the elders (spiritual leaders) of the church and they are to pray over him, anointing him with oil in the name of the Lord; and the prayer of faith will restore the one who is sick, and the Lord will raise him up; and if he has committed sins, he will be forgiven. Therefore, confess your sins to one another [your false steps, your offenses], and pray for one another, that you may be healed and restored. The heartfelt and persistent prayer of a righteous man (believer) can accomplish much [when put into action and made effective by God--it is dynamic and can have tremendous power]." JAMES 5:14-16 AMP

He prayed for her. She felt like a big load was taken off her heart and shoulders. The pastor did not give her the slightest impression that her husband had ever divulged the information to him. He really admired the sincerity in her narrative.

Jessica was radiant as she walked shoulder high out of the pastor's office. She called her husband and told him what she had just done. With a very deep sigh he responded, "I hope you did not paint me black? I will go to see him." She was very happy and radiant. Her husband returned home after his meeting with the pastor. He said, "I have a confession to make." She thought he was going to talk of any illicit relationship. "Almost a year ago, I met with the pastor and confessed my past and all that transpired before our wedding. I strongly pleaded with him never to divulge the information. I am happy he kept his words without allowing the information affect his relationship with us." Jessica was very sobered by the experience. She realized why her husband was radiant while she was still under the torment of guilt. She had a good respect for the pastor. She rushed for her bible and opened to Prov. 14: 34-35. She read it aloud.

"Righteousness [moral and spiritual integrity and virtuous character] exalts a nation, but sin is a disgrace to any people. The king's favor and good will are toward a servant who acts wisely and discreetly, but his anger and wrath are toward him who acts shamefully." PROVERBS 14:34-35 AMP

Her husband embraced her and led a session of prayers.

At the end of her menstrual circle she realized she missed her usual frustrating menstruation. Her checkup showed that she was pregnant. She was shocked. She rushed home to give her husband the news because she forgot her phone at home. She opened the door with excitement and ran into her husband who greeted her with the news of a job offer. She was overwhelmed. She wept like a baby and sobbed as she said, "My dear, did you realize that the devil had stagnated us and wasted our fortunes in the past three years? His strategies were concealed from us. You gave him a whole year to waste my blood because you did not tell me you were going to or had confessed to the pastor. At this juncture, her husband. Joined her in the tear flow. They prayed together and thank the Lord for a great deliverance. It was a new beginning in their marriage.

CHAPTER SIX

REMOTE CONTROL

Remote control in this context means a super natural or diabolic force that has a hold on any individual. The "controller" may not necessarily be physically present but can remotely control the activities of the said individual. There must always be a link, either by genetic traits, blood or mutual covenant. This force becomes a third party in a relationship by proxy of the agent or demonic projections.

Titus thought all was over when he got married to his wife after the turbulent courtship. The wedding was well attended from all classes represented in the community. His mother-in-law was the chief opposer and extreme objector to the relationship between him and his trusted darling wife. To his mother-in-law, he was the least qualified to marry her daughter. He was well read but not in one of the popular fields of studies commonly acceptable to people in their community. He got his MFA in Fine and Applied Art with a specialty in pottery. Mrs. Kalimantan his mother-in-law could not understand what he wanted to achieve with such an odd specialty. Her other reason for objection was that Titus had had a baby born to him while he was in high school. He gave his life to Jesus while in college. His seriousness with his Christian profession of faith was another jam in the wheel of any rapport between them both. He was a "Saul" turned "Paul". She hated him with passion. In her imagination, her daughter was hypnotized or bewitched to have fallen in love with him.

Close and extended family members were engaged in plea for mercy and leniency for her to agree to show up at the wedding. She hated Titus additionally because he had the favor of her hated brother-in-law who stood in, instead of her late husband. She had her own choice for her daughter who had long been branded, "terrestrial-disconnect" because of her Christian profession of faith. Her uncle did not believe in Jesus. The family religious believes hinged on liberality with a flair for the Islamic faith and traditional mode of worship. He however was an adherent to religious liberty. He believed that the religious faith of a female child would be determined by her husband.

Melissa had always proved to be a very faithful Christian and a reliable wife. Her husband had a very high level confidence in her. She was "his heartbeat." She had never been rude to her husband. Few months into the wedding, she could not account for her touchy and edgy response to virtually almost every action or inaction of her husband. She spent quality time praying on these unending ill-feelings against him. She was reluctant to share her experience with him. It was a growing distaste that she could not account for. Her husband had noticed the negative development of disconnect but could not lay his hands on any reason for his observations or conviction. She had a dream in which her mother was chasing her around with the scold that she had been a recalcitrant child. She woke up panting for breath. Her husband was scared. He bombarded her with multiple questions which were evident of his fears. She narrated her experience. With his hands laid on her head and her belly, he prayed aggressively. His prayer was of imprecations at anyone or agent of darkness that may be the source of attack on his darling wife. The prayer session was interrupted by a phone call. The caller-id showed the name of his mother-in-law. He refrained her from answering the call. He picked the call with the traditional "Hello Ma." "I did not call for you but my daughter." His mother-in-law responded. "Ok Mom, I will hand her the phone." He called his wife and handed her the phone. She was still in the frenzy of her scary dream.

She spoke inadvertently of her scary dream. She said, "Mom, why are you chasing me? I just woke up from a scary dream in which you were pursuing me. I guess I do not need this, this time around." Her mother was shocked. She responded, "I am not the one pursuing you, it must be your mother-in-law and those who hated my sincere declaration about your 'liability' of a husband." Melissa was offended especially because the phone was on speaker. Titus was not offended but prepared to turn the intention of his mother-in-law into foolishness. He heard her say, "I have told you not to marry that liability, and whatever you experience with him is your doing against yourself. Has he brought in his 'attaché'?" Referring to the seven year old daughter of Titus. The regular reference to Titus as a liability by his mother-in-law was a big challenge to him. He determined to prove her wrong. He remembered he once heard his friend tell him, "Critics do not determine the fate of the criticized, but the attitude of the criticized does."

The telephone conversation was over. Melissa, with tears rolling down her cheeks embraced her husband to tender an apology on behalf of her mother. He wiped the tears off her face with the palm of his hands. He gave her the assurance of his love. "Listen my darling, I shall never be discouraged or develop any cold feet about our relationship. For your information, your mother's criticism has become my inspiration. I will by the grace of God prove her wrong. By the grace of God I will not be negatively influenced by any human factor. I remain yielded to the control of the Holy Spirit." His wife was highly impressed that he did not take any offense against her or her mother. She assured him she would keep her promise to take good care of Tina, with whom she had bonded in the course of their courtship. To herself she said, "This is a man to whom I will remain faithful till death do us part. I am now very sure my mother does not wish me well in this relationship."

Her thoughts reflected on her face. Her husband approached her and said. "Let not your heart be troubled, we are in this together. We are not alone, the Lord is on our side. We shall be like Mt. Zion that shall not be moved." Melissa became pregnant. She was confused because she still had partial blood spotting during her regular menstrual circles for the first two months. She sensed some changes in her body coupled with 'morning sickness'. They visited the clinic and it was confirmed that she was about three months pregnant. She determined not to let her mother know about the pregnancy. Two days after the clinic confirmation, her phone rang. It was her mother. They had a "good" conversation which her mother ended with the statement, "There is nothing hidden under the heavens, pregnancy has a way of announcing itself. Her response was, "May it announce itself in our lives soonest in the mighty name of Jesus Christ. She waited for her mother to end the call. She left the call on for a long while but her mother refused to end the call. She kept the phone on as she walked away to the restroom. She came back, realized that her mother eventually ended the call. She concluded that her mother was tele-guiding and trying to remote control her. She narrated the experience to her husband. He was very angry but chose not to be infuriated by the whole experience. He told his wife that she needed to realize that a battle line has been drawn in the realm of the spirit. He said he was aware of the possibility of something like this since her mother insisted on her obstructive obstinacy on the issue of their relationship.

Spiritual warfare was set in motion. Melissa could not understand why her mother should be against her. She believed beyond any reasonable doubt that her experience was not ordinary. She believed she needed divine protection against any demonic insinuation or projection. They both joined their hands and prayed some very dangerous prayers. They asked the Lord to reveal all the secret plans of the devil and cast any enemy or agent of the devil against their marriage on the bed of affliction as stated in the book of revelation. At the end of the prayer session they were both drenched in sweat. They looked at each other's face. Titus said to his wife, "...thank God for the present challenges. It has gotten us closer to each other and God. I do not pray we face challenges all our lives, but if our experience in the past few days kept us spiritually fit, I would love to live fired-up all my life." "I pray we remain fired-up but challenges should cease in the mighty name of Jesus Christ." His wife responded. Great 'Aaameen' roared from Titus.

A phone call was received by Titus from his mother-in-law. She was very hostile and threatening. He questioned her, "Mom, what is my offense?" "It is not your fault but my rodent that chose to swim in your pond." She hung the phone. He could not get over the experience but he refused to inform his wife about the development. His wife noticed his sudden cold attitude and non-communication. She pressed him to no avail to compel him to divulge the information. "Your joy is my pursuit, my mouth shall not destroy my desire." His wife suspected that he must have had a brush with her mother. She determined not to press any further, lest her peace be disturbed. They both were in good agreement on most issues except on acceptance of their parents.

Melissa loved her mother very much and would not want to agree that she would work against her. She was torn between two walls. She had every reason to believe the obvious but the age long bond she had had with her mom was difficult to break. She was overwhelmed with sorrow. She burst into tears and was gracefully comforted by her husband to whom she could not disclose the very cause of her pain. They prayed together as they went to bed. The pregnancy was doing well, but Melissa occasionally experienced threatened abortion in her dream. It got to a point that she could not keep it to herself any longer. She informed her husband. His response was, "you both have been my prayer point, and I am fully persuaded you will deliver safely.

Titus' mom had a very scary dream about her daughter-in-law. Considering her state of gestation, she chose to tell the dream to her son. Titus was scared to the skin of his teeth. His mother promised to join him and his wife in serious prayers to avert the plans of the devil. The key text he used in prayers was: Exodus 23:26, Isaiah 56:3-7, Deut. 7:14, Isaiah 66:8, Gen. 9: 7... Melissa being a darling daughter-in-law to Titus' Dad, he could not keep his prayer points from her. He took his phone and called his daughter-in-law. "Hello my daughter and my wife. How is the baby doing? You have been the subject of our prayers. You will deliver safely. Every agent of complications will die in their own complications. I will bend my knees until I lift my grandchild from you. You shall live to enjoy the fruit of your labor. Every unrepentant enemy of your soul will pay with their lives. The psalmist says, *"I shall not die, but live, And declare the works of Jehovah."* Psa. 118:17 ASV.

You shall live to see good days and attend my funeral. By the grace of God, He has assured me that I will not die until I reach a ripe old age. You will surely deliver safely, in Jesus' mighty name." Melissa shouted a resounding amen. She however questioned, "Grandpa, why were you this desperate and precise on praying for my life." "The devil is a liar. Matthew 18: 19 says,

"Verily I say unto you, what things soever ye shall bind on earth shall be bound in heaven; and what things soever ye shall loose on earth shall be loosed in heaven. Again I say unto you, that if two of you shall agree on earth as touching anything that they shall ask, it shall be done for them of my Father who is in heaven." Matthew 18:18-19 ASV.

We have prayed and all is settled in the presence of the Lord. In the mighty name of Jesus." Her father-in-law replied.

Melissa was disturbed, she shared with her husband the experience of her prayer session with his father. Titus was not too pleased with the fact that his father shared the scary divine information with her. He said, "We are victorious. No evil shall befall us. We are in the hands of the Lord, the Bible says,

""For ye died, and your life is hid with Christ in God." Colossians 3:3 ASV *"For thus saith Jehovah of hosts: After glory hath he sent me unto the nations which plundered you; for he that toucheth you toucheth the apple of his eye."* Zechariah 2:8 ASV. Do not be afraid, God has not given us the spirit of fear but of power and of love and of a sound mind, as stated in 2Timothy 1: 7 Now that you know the warfare we are into, we are all on same page."" "That is fine, I know I shall deliver safely as the Lord revealed to me in my dream just yesterday." "Amen." Her husband responded.

The unity and love in the marriage of Titus and Melissa was a threat to the devil and a wall of protection to them. The mother of Melissa made a demonic projection on her daughter such that she was to see her husband as an enemy. The spell was catching on her intermittently. On some occasions, she wouldn't want to see her husband. She once told him that she doesn't feel secured around him. Some other unusual comments were initially taken as side effect of late pregnancy. The Holy Spirit prompted her husband not to take the issue as physical or ordinary. He shared his experience with his prayer partner. They went into intense prayer sessions. Few days thereafter Melissa told her husband what she had been struggling with. They prayed together and thank the Lord for victory. Melissa was feeling unusually funny. She called her pastor's wife to share her feelings with her. They were still on their conversation when her water broke. She told the pastor's wife that she just peed on herself. The experienced mother knew she was about to experience the onset of labor. She dashed down to meet with her. She encouraged her to endure the pain for a while before they called the ambulance for the hospital. She displayed a good resistance to pain. They headed for the hospital. She delivered like the Hebrew women. It was a baby boy. Titus was very excited because he was once told that the baby was a girl until another scan revealed the baby as a boy. He was not sure of which report to believe. He picked his phone to call his mother-in-law, but his phone rang, it was his mother-in-law. She called to apologize for her high handedness and series of insults. His response was, "Mommy, I really appreciate your apology. Mom, you got your grandchild come in just about five minutes ago. He is a boy. She was excited. She shouted a thunderous hallelujah. Titus was surprised that his mother-in-law could call him and apologize. Her excitement over the birth was another surprise because she was adjudged an enemy of their union. Many names were sent by the grandparents. His grandmother named him Reconciliation. The name was not the choice of the young parents. They however knew the implication of a decline or rejection of the name. They concluded to abbreviate the name. He was therefore named Reconciliation but popularly called Recon.

Things were very fine but for the unusual hatred that was breeding in the life of Titus against his wife. Her voice was made offensive to his ears. He reacted hostile to almost every of her inquests and requests. Their relationship became strained. Though she was not happy about the development, however she found solace in her son. Her attention and affection were shifted to her son. She enjoyed breastfeeding him because it gave her emotional satisfaction. Titus hated his hatred for his wife but could not explain what went wrong. She was rarely any longer sexually attractive to him. He knew something was wrong. He shared his experience with a friend that had read a book, "PASTOR'S WIFE PRAYING MANUAL" by Pastor Grace Okonrende on similar experience. He realized that he was being remotely controlled. He remembered the story of a brother who had illicit sexual relationship with a strange lady and was always hearing a whisper in his spirit to go to places only to discover that the lady was waiting out there to receive him. He likens his experience to such cases. He determined to meet his pastor for a deliverance ministration session. The deliverance was in session when a female voice started speaking through him. She claimed, "Titus is mine, he entered into a marriage covenant with me when we had our first sexual relationship. Does he think he can abandon me for any other woman and have peace. I will cost him this marriage. I have used Kally against them both to no avail. Kally is very ignorant of the fact that she sold herself to my boss when she nurtured bitterness against Titus. Melissa escaped my plans at childbirth. Ooooo...no. Look at this idiot, I will deal with you. Kally will come to take care of your baby, you will know you cannot get away from me. I will cost you this marriage." With a righteous indignation, the Pastor commanded the demon to go to the bottomless pit. Titus was flat on the floor foaming through the mouth. He was motionless and quiet. He was feared dead. Suddenly he opened his eyes. "Pastor why am I on the floor? Titus questioned. The pastor commanded him to stand on his feet. He stood up. He was made to confess Jesus as his Lord and savior. He was shown the recording of the ministration. The pastor asked, "...who is Kally?" "That is the nickname of my mother-in-law. She hates me with passion, but recently she called for reconciliation. The very day our baby was born." The pastor tried to clear the air on the personality of Mrs. Kalimantan. "Pastor, now that my mother in-law has become impersonated, what shall we do?" He questioned. The pastor suggested that both his wife and her mother should be shown the recording so that they could be freed from the remote control of the forces of darkness. "My mother-in-law will not agree to come for any deliverance. She is a fanatical Muslim. She had wanted to come since Recon was born but my wife insisted that she preferred my mother to be with her" "Now that you know she was under remote control to hate you and try to destroy your marriage. You have to pray for the salvation of her soul so that you can have peace in your home.

Grandma Kalimantan was very bitter over the decline of her proposal to come over to assist her daughter. Her spirit was grieved and through that the impersonating spirit made her to agree to do anything she could to retaliate or avenge herself. She called Titus and said, "I will stay in my husband's house as you suggested and not intrude into the affairs of your home. I thought of letting go of the past, but now I know you do not want me around you. Always remember you have my daughter as wife." The situation was very overwhelming for Titus. His pastor on hearing of the latest development gave him some words of assurance of faith. He was advised to read and pray with the following bible passages. Isaiah 54: 15-17, 1 John 4: 4. Zech. 2: 8. Isaiah 59: 19. Rom. 12: 18. The relationship between Melissa and her husband improved. The demonic influence on their relationship was terminated. They became very affectionate but could not resolve the contentions of Grandma Kalimantan. Titus after watching the recording of the deliverance agreed to work on her mother-in-law for the salvation of her soul. He realized that he needed to work on his personal spiritual life so that the forces of darkness whom he had exposed himself to in the past do not regain access into his life. It was good that Titus realized the implication of his past. He became more fervent with his Christian life. He read his bible regularly and would not cease to pray. His meditations were always on the scriptures. He got more involved in evangelism. He spent every day as it were his last.

He was prompted to respond to an advertisement he saw on one of the public newspapers. He applied and was offered a very good job by a ceramic factory as the chief creative artist and curator. It was a good opportunity for him to explore and exploit his gift and skill in ceramic technology. He was very successful in his researches. He designed May products that fetched the company a lot of income. The company promoted him into the position of director so as to keep him in the company. Titus realized he would do better if he established his own company. He however determined to gain more grounds in the company and the commerce world before embarking on such venture.

Money was no more an issue in the relationship between Melissa and her husband. As promised, Titus determined to win the heart of his mother-in-law. She was a principal subject of his prayers. He visited her at the end of the year with a very fat check. He wrote on the check, "For a gift of your choice." It was a gift she could not afford to decline. She had never received such a check in her entire life. She called her daughter to express her surprise. She was the more surprised when her daughter informed her that she was not aware that her husband gave her such an amount of money. "He only told me he was visiting you to express his love for the challenges you gave him for which he has been adequately rewarded. Yes I know that the Lord has rewarded him greatly. Currently he is almost the owner of the largest ceramic industry in the country. He told me he was going to give you a check for a gift of your choice. He tried to know what exactly you needed. We could not come to a conclusion. I however told him you once spoke about a remodel of your kitchen." "You mean he can afford the check he gave me..." "How much was the check?" "Please ask him yourself, I am still in shock. I am very sorry for all the evil I have wished him in my thoughts." "You probably exposed yourself to the devil to make you hate him, he really loves you," Melissa conclusively told her mother.

Titus invited his mother-in-law for a visit. It was a nice reunion. At a moment in the course of their discussion, Titus decided to show his mother-in-law the recording of his deliverance which he claimed was the source of their reconciliation. Grandma Kalimantan watched with utmost interest. She realized her personal bitterness for her son-in-law had exposed her to demonic impersonation and infestation. She requested to meet with the pastor for her personal freedom. It was the beginning of the journey for the salvation of her soul.

CHAPTER SEVEN

"THE AMERICAN GREEN-CARD"
[An infiltration]

It was a magnanimous move on the part of the government of America to initiate the Green-card Lottery Visa Program. A plus to America but brain-drain to many African and other nations given the "privilege". The sufferings of many Africans painted a picture of relief and deliverance from hardship. Timothy and his wife Celina were two of the lucky ones that won the visa lottery. His family was excited and started dreaming big of going to America. When the news got to Timothy's parents, they were well pleased, with the notion that they will surely get to America before they cross to the "great-beyond". Celina's parents were much younger but more eager to go abroad to make money before they were too old to run around with ambition.

There was a brief send-forth that they could barely afford after the purchase of the flight tickets. The journey was smooth but for one or two misconceptions. It was the first time the young couple was to be aboard an airplane though they were well read and graduates in their respective disciplines. They were completely ignorant of their right to a free meal during the flight. They ate very well before boarding because they could not afford additional expenses in the course of the journey. They declined the offer of meals or drinks in their attempt to save cost. However their "pre-loaded" meal was fully digested by the time they landed for their connecting flight to Houston from Amsterdam. Timothy turned to his lovely wife and said, "I guess you should be feeling hungry by now? Especially for your state." Celina was six months pregnant. She nodded her head in consent to his assertion. "Anyway, I am not feeling too bad because I am used to fasting," she replied. Timothy was not comfortable with the slightest discomfort of his wife. It was time to board the connecting flight. A few minutes after the take-off, an announcement was made that a meal will be served as soon as the plane reached a cruising level. Celina turned to her husband and questioned, "Do you have an idea of the cost?" "I guess I heard that it is complimentary," he said. "Please ask the hostess." Celina requested. "I don't have to. I guess everybody ahead of us has been served and none of them made a payment," he retorted. The meals were served, they both enjoyed it. Timothy was at peace but his wife was in anticipation of a bill. In the course of the journey, Celina needed an additional drink but she did not speak out until she could not bear it any longer. She whispered to her husband, "I am very thirsty.." Timothy called for two cups of orange juice and a cup of water which were freely and timely supplied. After the very refreshing experience the expectant mother turned to her husband and said, "I trust you for my comfort, please tell the hostess that I need another meal." Timothy was a little agitated. He said, "I knew the first meal was complimentary, but your requested additional meal may be charged." She smiled as she said to her husband, "I am sure you wouldn't mind spending a little more for your baby... anyway, don't worry, I can endure it. " "You don't have to, "he replied. He unstrapped himself and went straight to the air-hostess. He said, "Ma, sorry to burden you, my pregnant wife wants additional food." The air-hostess with a radiant smile said, "I know how it feels, I will surely come around to attend to her. I am sure you are responsible for this and you are ready to bear the full responsibility." She read the imagination of Timothy on his face and quickly added, we won't send you any bills unless you choose to pay my next salary." The statement made him smile. His wife was given additional meal at no cost. She was very grateful to the air-hostess, who was very friendly and shared pleasantries as she offered her services. They arrived in Houston safely. The pilot was well experienced, the landing was exceptionally pleasant, almost all of the passengers clapped their hands and congratulated themselves for a safe journey.

Timothy and Celina Macaulay were heartily received by their host. It was the beginning of a new experience. After a deep breath, Celina commented, "The air here is very fresh...who cursed Africa?" They all laughed, it was a smooth ride to the residence of the Briggs. Timothy and his wife were captivated by the interlocking overhead bridges and the beautifully lit skyscrapers that made the skyline very fascinating and attractive. "This city is beautiful," Celina soliloquized. "You are welcome to America," Mr. Briggs responded.

Mrs. Florence Briggs was home making ready the dinner for her guests. It was a nice time to share the memories of their high school days. They all attended the same school as there were not too many high schools in their community. The Briggs put them through all the necessary paperwork. In a few weeks they were settled and fairly integrated into the system. They soon realized that their academic certificates from Africa could not fetch them any professional job. They had to do some odd jobs pending the validation of their certificates so they could enroll for some adaptation courses or challenge the boards in their respective fields. Besides the continuous assessment, they found the academic experience in America a little easier. It was a complete departure from the "all-mighty-June," a one-time sessional examination they were used to back home.

The pressure was mounting from their parents and siblings. They were shocked by the fact that the Dollar was not readily available for them to spend in America. Timothy was angry when his wife was accused of not allowing him to fulfill his promises of sending a car to his parents. He had just survived the basic cost of the delivery of Tom their first child. He was struggling to find a way around other associated outstanding bills because they had no personal health insurance policy in place. He told his younger brother, "There is no Dollar producing tree in America. The popular "Dollar Tree" is the name of a trading store. If there was, any Dollar yielding tree in America, they must all have died before our arrival in this country. Please don't ever accuse or charge my wife for my inability to fulfill my promises. She is the only one working to keep us going." The message was not relayed to his parents in a friendly manner. It actually deepened the distaste that his mother had for his wife. Celina had to work very hard to pay all the bills and the daycare center while Timothy was in school for his adaptation courses. He was able to pass his examinations but could not easily get a good job. He had to revert to doing odd jobs pending the time he found a professional career. He went to his job in anger almost every day. He contemplated changing his phone number so as to avoid the pressure of his parents and siblings. Celina would not allow him to do anything against the interest of his parents as she was very aware that she would be the one assumed to be responsible for any ill-fated experience on the part of her in-laws. Any phone call from back home was received with anger in anticipation of a request for assistance or demand for the fulfillment of a promise earlier made. A call came in from Timothy's younger brother. Timothy decided to speak 'Spanish' to give the impression of a wrong number. Celina was watching her husband in amazement as he spoke a language he did not understand at least to the level of having a conversation. She was the more surprised and shocked when her husband burst into laughter after dropping the call. "What is funny?" "It was a call from Frank. I had to reply in "SPANISH." I heard my parents speaking in the background, asking him what I said. He told them the response was in a different language. They blamed him for calling a wrong number. He assured them that he was sure he called the right number. He said, "Mom, I have the number in my notebook," That was the last statement he made before hanging up the phone." Celina was very angry with her husband. She knew she would incur the displeasure of her in-laws if they were not able to get the desired response from him. She turned to him and said, "I am sure, or let me say I believe you do not want to get me into trouble with your people, especially your Mom!" It was not a pleasant discussion as Celina promised to tell his parents about his pretense. She pointed out the spiritual implication of his action, that it implied a lie. Timothy could not contend her assertion. He determined not to fall a victim of Satan's ploy to lying. At the close of the discussion it was agreed that the "fooling-exercise" should not be disclosed. In closing he said, "You better pray very well that I get a professional career job if you don't want me to speak 'mandatory-Spanish.' They both laughed as Celina departed for her night shift.

Five years had passed before the Macaulay was qualified to be sworn in as citizens of America. Their citizenship qualified them to file for green-card on behalf of their parents. Celina chose to be quiet on the question of who to invite first. Timothy was very inclined on getting his mother to come over to the USA. He had gotten a professional job that afforded him a very good salary. Celina was able to go back to school to study for a degree in nursing. They had just closed on a new residential building that was custom-built to their taste. They already had a boy and a girl and agreed to stop "biological-evangelism." If there was any reason why Celina would have her mother-in-law come around, it was all about babysitting or care for their two children. The arrangement was made and Grandma Macaulay was on her way to the USA. Timothy was on duty so Celina was to pick her mother-in-law from the airport. She did her due diligence. The food was made ready before she left the house for the airport. She prayed for divine favor on their meeting. She was at the arrival gate thirty minutes before the scheduled landing time of the flight. Her time consciousness saved her from what would have turned out to be an embarrassment because the flight came much earlier than expected. She was at the gate for less than ten minutes when her mother-in-law walked through. It was a nice reunion as she had never gone back to Africa in almost six years. Her traditional mode of welcome called for the focus of all bystanders. Her mother-in-law felt honored as every eye seemed to suggest she was a dignified personality. "Where is Timothy?" Her mother-in-law questioned. "He had to go to work, the children are in the daycare center and school respectively while I have to take time off school to come to receive you ma," she narrated.

They went straight to the car park and in a few minutes they were on their way home. They talked about a lot of things as she carefully drove. She determined to win the mind of her mother-in-law during what she saw as an opportunity. They had never sat alone together for ten minutes since the relationship between them started. She was busy talking as a tour guide, explaining where they were and the significance of every imposing structure or monument. She made a lot of good promises and assurances on how she would make her stay in America a pleasant one. Grandma Macaulay was very impressed. She blamed herself for her undue reservations against her. However, deep down in her heart she had the feelings that Celina had stolen the heart of her son. She loved to be in company and in control of her son. The house was about an hour to the airport but the journey was prolonged due to heavy traffic as it was closing time for most workers driving home from the city center. Celina made a lasting impression on her mother-in-law. They arrived home safely. She briskly conducted her mother-in-law through the beautiful five bedroom house. She looked around with awe. She wondered how her son lived as a king in America and had not responded commensurately to their demands and incessant requests. She put all the blame on Celina whom she adjudged as lazy and a liability to her son. Celina engaged her with the African news station while she put the already prepared meal into the microwave oven. Everything came out very hot. The table was set. Grandma Macaulay was surprised how within few minutes such a delicious meal was made ready. Her eyes were all over the beauty of the home, especially the drapery on the high ceiling windows with the fascinating scalloping. She felt it was all a waste of funds while they struggled for survival back in Africa. She inquisitively questioned Celina on the cost of the decorations. She was tactful in her response. She claimed it was the prerogative of her husband. She encouraged her mother-in-law to bless the food and eat. She opened the dishes and attempted to serve but was restrained by her mother-in-law. "You have done well, please allow me to serve myself." Celina took the gesture of decline as casual and a ploy. She insisted to serve. Her service was allowed and later acknowledged with dignity. The sumptuous dinner was another offense against Celina. Her crime was that the quantity of the meat, fish and shrimp was too wasteful.

Gazing at the wall clock, she took permission from her mother-in-law that she would have to rush out to the daycare center to bring home the children. She escorted her mother-in-law to her designated bedroom. Everything was sparkling and elegant. She dashed out of the house in haste as she was far beyond the pickup time. She returned home and

Grandma was fast asleep. She was woken up by the grand children who snuck into her room to check on her. She was forced to wake up by the very curious toddler. She was excited to see her grandchildren but felt her daughter-in-law should have prevented them from disturbing her sleep. She put the toddler on the side of the wall as they both slept off. After a few minutes, the toddler woke up and climbed over her grandmother to reach out for her mother. She fell in the process and landed on her right hand. The sound of her fall and incessant cry woke her grandma and got the attention of her mother. It was discovered that she cried the more whenever her right arm was touched. Celina was scared of a fractured bone. She had just driven off on her way to the hospital when her husband drove into the driveway of the house. He entered into the house to find his mother in a very sober mood. Their joy of reunion was tinctured with gloom over the accident. His mother narrated the scenario in a way that put the blame on his wife. She claimed it was not right for Celina to bring or allow the children into her room while she was already asleep and that she must have called for Tammy, an action that was believed to have prompted the toddler to jump over her while she was asleep. The narrative did not win the fancy of Timothy. His concern was about the state of the health of his daughter.

He called Celina's number and the phone rang on the dining table. She had forgotten it in the panic and frenzy of the moment. Timothy's phone rang and it was his wife on the line. She had borrowed somebody's phone to make the call. "How is Tammy?" He questioned. "She has a sprain on her right arm, she must have landed on her elbow that actually caused a strain in the ligament and sprained the ulna and radius. The X-ray did not show any fracture. The doctor said it will heal with time. She was given an injection to relieve her of the pain. A prescription was also written for me to pick up at the pharmacy near our house," she explained.

Timothy determined not to share his mother's narrative with his wife. He suspected the report was self-exonerating to the discredit of his wife. In his understanding, a divulge of such information would do more harm than good in the family. Celina returned home with her daughter. Interestingly Tammy gravitated towards her grandma and was so handed over by her mother. The maturity of Timothy actually paid off. Celina did not show any offense but her mother-in-law looked awfully worried. The entire house was unusually calm and suggestive of tension. Celina sensed that something must have gone wrong but could not imagine any other development but the fall of Tammy. She turned to her mother-in-law and said, "Grandma, please do not get worried or disturbed about the fall of Tammy, it is one of the challenges with toddlers, they get excited and adventurous when they meet people they had longed for." Timothy quickly cut in to prevent his mother from trying to explain anything about how the accident occurred. His interception was a safety valve. Celina was able to read between the lines that her husband was not going to allow his mother to talk on the issue. She could not advance any particular reason. It was bedtime, Tammy already slept off in her grandma's arms. Grandma called on Celina to come for Tammy. The two children were put in bed by their mother.

Timothy had to leave the house much earlier than usual because of a scheduled meeting in his office. His mother was surprised that he had left the house before she woke up. Celina had dressed the children ready for school and daycare center respectively. She turned to her mother-in-law and said, "Grandma, I am taking the children to school and I will from there go to my own school as well." As she was about to step out of the house, she turned back to teach her mother-in-law how to operate the video player and the television to keep her busy. She got the children into the car and drove off. After about two hours, Grandma Macaulay felt bored by the entire setting. She stepped out of the house to see if she could find any of the neighbors to talk to. She felt out of place. She returned into the house to try her hands on the electronic gadgets. After some frantic efforts, she was able to figure out how to handle the various gadgets. She watched as many movies as she could, slept and woke up, she went out again to find someone to chat with. She found the next door neighbor. With great excitement, she greeted her expecting a good response. She was shocked by the miserly-smile that she got in response. She went back into the house and determined to sleep for the remaining hours of the day to avoid boredom.

At about 6:30pm. Celina strolled into the house with her children and went into Grandma's room to inform her that she was back. The children were excited to see their grandma again. They were all over her. Celina asked her about how her day had been. Her countenance said it all. She shook her head in dismay of the setting of things in the neighborhood. She said, "Is this what life is like here in America? Do you do this every day? Life could be too boring to idle hands and too challenging for able hands that are gainfully engaged. I watched more than enough movies for my liking." With a smile she responded, "This is exactly the life of average first generation immigrants in America. My husband needs be on his job for me to go to school. I have had to work for the past four years for him to go to school. Thank God he passed his exams in good grades to afford him the privilege of his current job which made it possible for us to be creditworthy to buy this house, his car and the furnishings, all on credit. I have to be in school so that I can improve myself so as to get a professional job that we may get out of these debts that had kept us running from pillar to post." After a deep breath her mother-in-law embraced her and said, "God will be with you and see you through, my daughter." She was very impressed that she was addressed as a 'daughter' by her mother-in-law.

The children would gravitate more towards their grandmother because they get away with some of their naughtiness and antics. Another reason was because she spent more time with them than their parents did. She stayed home with them while their parents pursued their desired goals. Celina and her mother-in-law were both careful in their dealings. She had always been the one that took her out to most places she ever desired to go. Most of the time she opted to sit at the back of the car for the safety of the children and to curb their sibling rivalry.

One Sunday morning it was agreed that the entire family would go to church in Timothy's car.

Grandma Macaulay on her own decided to sit at the passenger's seat in the front. Her intention was to have a good feel of the car and easy access to her son. Celina came out and saw her sitting in the passenger's seat. She carefully went back into the house to inform her husband. It was a challenging situation for Timothy. He wanted to go tell his mother to go to the back seat but was cautioned by the Holy Spirit not to do so but to allow his wife do the driving while he seats with the children at the back. He turned to his wife and said, "Now that grandma is sitting in the front, you will have to do the driving." She did not like it, but had no better idea to avert a strife. They were about to set out when grandma exploded in rage against her son, "Ahaa, why should your wife be the one to drive. Are you not the man. Celina was about to burst but her husband quickly cut in to say, "It is a women's world today. Celina quickly borrowed a smile from the Holy Spirit. The ride to church was smooth but quiet.

The sermon of the day was as if the pastor knew what happened in the car. He spoke about love, tolerance, unhealthy rivalry and divided interest. At a point he mentioned rivalry between mother-in-laws and their daughter-in-laws. The whole church burst into laughter as the pastor demonstrated the prayers of some daughter-in-laws. He demonstrated their gesticulations at the place of prayers asking God to "kill...,terminate..." He closed his little dramatic session with the statement, "Your mother-in-laws or father-in-laws will not die in Jesus' name...Your son-in-law and your daughter-in-law shall prosper to the glory of God in Jesus' name." There was a resounding amen across the church. Timothy was contemplating how to handle the circumstance he found himself in. Before they headed for the car he spoke to his mother, Mom, I guess it will be proper that you sit at the back with your grandchildren, they are always wanting to be around you." His mother was sharp to reply, "Am I their mother, their mother should live up to her responsibility. I am not sitting at the back. If that is the plan between you and your wife, go back to her and inform her that I declined." He was shocked. He could not understand why his mother seemed not to have listened to the sermon of the pastor. He tendered apologies. He went to his wife and handed her the car-key. Celina was not aware of any misunderstanding between Timothy and his mother. She just assumed it was a conformity with the setting of things. As they got on the street, she suggested that they should all go to a restaurant for lunch. To Timothy, the idea sounded good. She turned to her mother-in-law and expressed the idea of making her have a taste of American buffet. Grandma Macaulay responded, "Do you dictate to your husband what to be done? It is not your fault but that of a man that has lost his rightful position."

There was silence in the car. Celina was in a shock. She carefully pulled to the side of the road and exited into the next available parking lot. She told her husband that she had a panic attack. Her hands were shaking, she could not say a word in response to her mother-in-law's statements. She got out of the car and asked her husband to do the driving. Timothy looked into the eyes of his wife with an unspoken apology but a look that said, "I am sorry, just don't say a word." Timothy got into the driver seat and headed to one of the best restaurants. He turned to his mother and said, "Mom, this is one of the most prestigious restaurants in the city of Houston. I had thought of it immediately after the service, interestingly Celina probably read my mind and beat me to the suggestion. I would have suggested it if she was just a minute delayed in making the suggestion." His mother replied with a deep sigh, "Continue your cover-up, you may go into the restaurant but I will remain in the car with the children." "No Mom, the children will come with us. It is a family lunch. We all have to go in," he said. Celina was very disappointed by the developments. She knew that the devil was up to something. She remembered her pastor's counsel at moments of offense. *"Borrow any of the necessary fruit and gifts of the spirit that will keep you in line with the will of the Lord."* She turned to her mother-in-law and said, "Grandma, please let's go in, you will like it. We do not come here often, the idea is to actually give you a treat. I am not a certified chef as the people in there. My consolation and edge is the fact that they do not cook African dishes." Her mother-in-law was beaten hands-down. She agreed and came out of the car. She walked in the direction of her son while leaving her grandchildren at the back seat of the car. Their mother was seriously offended. She determined to keep her children away from her mother-in-law. Timothy was very disappointed in his mother. He felt she was out to get his wife and intended to strain their relationship. Celina decided to do the driving from the restaurant to their home. As soon as she got into the car, her mother-in-law asked whether she was okay enough to drive. Celina was speechless. She drove home carefully. She went to her mother-in-law on her knees appealing for forgiveness for any offense over her silence on the way home. Her mother-in-law called her husband to come and raise his wife off the ground. He declined the invitation without a word as he strolled into his bedroom. Celina got off her knees and went straight to be with her children. Tom was already asleep on his bed while little Tammy was lying on her father's chest in the master-bedroom. She was not sure whether to talk to her husband or not. Timothy's greetings expressed his innocence and Celina was able to think straight on all that was going on. She asked her husband, "What exactly did I do wrong?" "If you actually did anything wrong, not that I know of," her husband replied. "There is no doubt, the devil is seriously at work. Please speak to your mom to let peace reign," she requested.

Timothy felt torn between two walls. He decided to speak to his pastor about the conflicting situation. Before then, he tried to find out where and when things went wrong between his mother and his wife. He found a good time to discuss with his mother, a time when his wife was out of the house. He went into his mother's room, greeted her and offered her a bottle of malt, knowing it was her favorite drink. "My darling son, thank you for this drink. I cannot imagine that you have it in this country," she gratefully expressed. "Yes we have many African stuff made available at the designated stores." Timothy was very sober as he asked his mother what exactly his wife did wrong. "Was that a question or a confirmation that she did everything wrong? I have watched carefully the way everything was going since I came. Is she your husband and controller? Whoever did the Cham for her to enslave you will have to realize that I am here to deliver you. I have heard her call you by name on many occasions. Was she there when you were named. I would never have thought that it is possible for someone to enslave you. She doesn't work but will decide what you should spend your hard earned money on. What was wrong with her that she could not get to prepare food for you and the children after the service on Sunday afternoon? Only to decide, *"We should go to the restaurant."* Even if she is pregnant, is the fetus in her palm? I cannot believe what you have become ...sheepish and subordinate... Huuunnn. Well, it is your choice and your life, however I will put her in her rightful position now that I am around." Timothy felt he had heard more than enough. He looked straight into his mother's eyes and said, "Mom, you are making a very great mistake, you are biting the fingers that fed you. I guess your ingratitude is based on my error to have made you ignorant of the source of all the benefits you got in our first five years of coming into this country. Celina had been the breadwinner of the family until I finished my academic programs that afforded me my current job. Please as much as possible avoid any contention with her. She has never done you any evil. She has instigated all the benefits you enjoyed from this family. She insisted that we should invite you to come. If she had insisted on having her mother come before you, I would not have objected. Please do not stress my wife." Looking at him snobbishly she sarcastically said, "See, a man in a skirt. You had better exchanged your masculinity for femininity so that you may be called a good husband. By the way, who asked her to invite me first, such that you now paint a picture of something ever unheard of? Well it is not too late, she can ask me to go back to my country so that she can bring her mother to her "HAVEN." "Timothy was so enraged that he said, "Mom, I think you actually have to go back to your country." "She laughed hysterically as she said, "I told you, and the charms are actually working on you. It is of a fact that your head has been exchanged for something else..." He walked out of the room in rage, stormed into his bed room and slammed the door as if his mother was pursuing him. He yelled like a hyena as he vested his anger by punching a hole through the Sheetrock wall. Celina who had barely entered the bedroom was scared. She screamed, "what is all these?" She had never seen her husband in such a fit of anger. He was shaking. His wife chose to be quiet and motionless to allow the 'storm' to subside. She turned to him and said, "Please be careful, look at the damage you did to the wall. I can understand your plight, please calm down. Grandma will learn to live with us without the devil having his way." Timothy looked straight at the door shut behind him and burst into tears. She was able to read his mind and the probable cause of his tears. She said, "I know grandma got you enraged, whatever must have happened, please do your best to curtail your anger. At least what you did to the wall is enough for me to learn my lesson not to get you off." A smile of repentance ran across his face as he promised his wife that he would never be that enraged against her. She humorously added, "It was good that you left grandma's room...anyway, you wouldn't have caused us to call 911." His smile was broader when he said, "Except I lost my mind. She almost got me there. I had to vent my anger and pain" "Thank God! Not on me but the wall," she interrupted, rushed him with a passionate kiss that made it a good-night. Her kiss gave him reassurance of love both for him and his mother. He gave her the best of his strength until she asked for "the shower-of-blessings." It was a therapy that disarmed the devil.

She turned to her husband to ask of what grandma said that actually got him enraged. He responded out of his tiredness, he was slurring his words like a drunk. He slept off in her embrace. Though she acknowledged his tiredness that afforded her fulfillment, she believed that he was not prepared to share with her all that transpired in grandma's room. He woke up in the morning and rolled to his wife's side of the bed, woke her up with a kiss. She drew him in and embraced him. There was a knock on their bedroom door, it was grandma. She said, "I just want to say good morning and sorry for whatever happened yesterday." Celina was quiet, it was Timothy that responded, "Thank you mom, I will see you soon. I need to get ready for work." With a gentle whisper, Celina said, "Which of the works, me, your job or all of the above?" "You see, her apology burst my bubble and deflated my "tires". I think she will have to go back to her husband. She must have missed him," he jokingly responded in whisper. They both laughed as Timothy said, "I must resume both jobs immediately to balance my accounts." They had a nice time and set out for their regular daily routines.

Grandma had always offered to assist Celina in the aspect of cooking but not in the regular chores. Celina had always declined but she did not have any other options especially because her final examinations were fast approaching. She had the notion that her mother-in-law wanted to actually take over her kitchen. She determined to take the risk and ready for the battle when the examinations were done with. Grandma, a strong choleric would only agree to what she chose to do and when she chose to do it.

Celina happened to be a Sanguine while her husband was a Melancholic by temperament. She said to her husband, "Can I ask grandma to make the dinner for tonight? I just have to stay a little longer in the library. "Huunnm..." Her husband sighed. "You know the implication of that. If you tell her she will not agree. If I ask for it, she will take over your kitchen and probably determine what we eat. Which of the two options would you want to go with?" "For now let her take over the kitchen, at least it will grant me the opportunity to face my studies squarely," she responded. "You will need a crash helmet if you want it back before she returns to her husband or on her subsequent visits. You know she likes cooking," he cautioned. "Let's wait till then," she responded. Timothy stylishly asked his mother whether she would be willing to prepare one of those traditional African dishes for the family that evening. Her response was, "How do we get the ingredients?" "Oh...that is not a problem. I will tell 'your-wife' to take you to the grocery store," he responded. "Did you tell her about this your request?" He nodded and headed for the bedroom. He told his wife that the plan worked. She accompanied him to express her appreciation for the kind gesture of her mother-in-law. Grandma Macaulay boastfully said, "You will visit Nigeria tonight." They all wore radiant smiles.

Celina and her mother-in-law headed for the African grocery store. Every necessary ingredient was picked off the shelves. Grandma suggested that ingredients should be bought for subsequent meals. Celina agreed to all the necessary purchases. The cart was full. At the checkout point, the cashier asked whether Celina would want any cash back. She requested for cash back of sixty Dollars. As grandma Macaulay and her daughter-in-law drove off from the parking lot, she turned to Celina and whispered, "This your country is very good and nice, we bought all these items we did not pay and the cashier still gave us money back." With a smile she replied, "They already took the money out of our account through the plastic card you saw me give the lady cashier." "Hennn" Her Mother-in-law exclaimed. The journey home was very interactive.

A wonderful dinner was prepared. Celina was not home yet when her husband returned. He requested for dinner to be served. His mother suggested that they wait for Celina's return home. Timothy picked his phone and called his wife. She responded that they may go on with the dinner because she may not come back home until the next one and a half hour. Grandma was a little upset. She asserted that Celina deliberately stayed behind because she did the cooking. "Nooooo, she is studying for her exams," Timothy explained. They were still deliberating on exactly what to do when the phone rang. It was Celina. She said, "I am on my way home to join you at dinner probably before you are done" "We are in actual fact about to start the 'demolitions,' her husband jokingly responded. "Ok, tell grandma that I am coming in with my 'bulldozer' to do justice to the 'mountains." In a few minutes Celina was at the door. It was a wonderful evening.

The children commended the 'taste of Africa.' Celina unequivocally told them that it was grandma's idea and cooking. Timothy cut in to say it was not grandma's idea but his. "You killed the elephant with your mouth but Grandma fired the bullet," Celina retorted. Their son Tom, cut in with a chant, "... go grandma, go grandma, go grandma. Grandma is the best cook in the whole wide world..." Celina teased Tom to remember her cooking. The little boy raised his thumb up and chanted, "... go mommy, go mommy, but grandma is the greatest and best cook in the whole wide world. Little Tammy also joined his brother in the chant, "... go gyanma..." Celina humorously added, "From now your grandma will cook your food and when she goes back to Africa you will go with her." Tom was sober. His grandma said to him, "I am not going back soon and if I have to go back, I will happily take you with me.

Tom was very sad and started to cry. His father questioned him on why he suddenly started to cry, "I don't want to go to Nigeria, is Nigeria not Africa? My teacher showed us a video of how they killed people in Nigeria. I think that is why grandma escaped to be with us here in America." His parents were shocked about the impression their son had of his father's homeland. Tom turned to his mom and said, "Mommy, you are the best mother in the whole wide world." Grandma could not hold back her laughter. "It's not funny, please do not take me with you to Africa. Do all the cooking of Africa in America," the boy snapped. His mother pulled him to herself with the assurance that Grandma will not take him to Africa especially his father's home country Nigeria.

They spent the night explaining and showing him beautiful pictures of Africa, Nigeria in particular. After the explanations and beautiful pictures, he turned to his father and asked, "If Africa is that beautiful, why have you not travelled there or taken me there and why, my grandma does not want to go back soonest and my grandpa was mad for not allowing him to come here. You remember you were talking about armed robbers that killed people in houses in Nigeria." His parents were speechless. They both realized that they actually underrated the intelligence of the little lad. They felt guilty of talking ill of their home country in the presence of their children.

Cooking was exciting to Grandma Macaulay but she was very lazy with cleanup after cooking. In no time the kitchen was turned upside down. The stoves had a lot of dirts and evident of burnt food stuff. Celina could not complain and determined to endure everything till after her exams. She was able to study hard enough to come out in flying colors. On her graduation day she was accorded special honor as the valedictorian. After the ceremony she gave the scroll to her mother-in-law and asked her to wear her graduation gown as a mark of appreciation of her moral support during the most crucial times in her studies. Grandma Macaulay was very impressed. She watched the video of the occasion as if it was actually her own graduation ceremony.

Celina understudied her mother-in-law's style and skill at cooking. She realized that she wanted to always determine and influence her decisions. She expressed her observations to her husband. They both agreed that they should not argue with her on any issue but to bring such issues to the bedroom for final decisions. Celina got a very good job. Her salary was actually higher than that of her husband. They had no financial challenges. They agreed to share a bank account with individual financial liberty on designated spending limit.

Grandma was in full control of the kitchen. Celina had done all she could to regain the control of her kitchen to no avail. Many a times, grandma would have prepared a dish of her choice without any prior communication with her daughter-in-law. Celina explained her dilemma to her husband. He was very reluctant to get involved. He reminded his wife of his caution at the inception of the idea. She was however tactless in her response to her husband's reference to his cautionary notes two years ago. She sneered at him and said, "Would you want your mom to be our permanent cook?" She made the statement before she thought of its implication. "Did you not plan to make her one in the first place? I knew this day would come, and here it is. I have told you, you will need a helmet to get back your kitchen." She felt ridiculed. She was however able to hear the wisdom and whisper of the Holy Spirit, "Tell him he is your crash helmet." She jumped on his neck aggressively but in love and apologized for her unguarded statement. She pled for forgiveness with the explanation that she never at any point in time thought of making his mother a cook in their home. She whispered, "You are my 'crash helmet'." Her husband burst into laughter and said, "I guess your 'helmet' is not strong enough for the battle you prepared to fight." She laughed and humorously added, "You better call on your allies to help you because you are my shield and the crown of my head." Timothy was beaten beyond his wildest imagination. He could not but agree that his wife was operating under the influence of the Holy Spirit. With a broad smile he said, "We shall fight the battles together."

CHAPTER EIGHT

"THE NIGHTMARE"
[The danger of influence]

Anthony and Jemima were "gold-diggers" that hit the goldmine. On arrival in the United Kingdom, life was very rough and tough for them both. They only communicated with their people back home in Africa through phone or handed letters. It was such a struggle that completely changed their ways of life. They realized the authenticity of the old adage that states, ***"Poverty isolates its victims, and affluence associates its possessors."*** When things were rough, they could not travel back to Africa. Besides the expensive travel ticket, the expectations of their old-time friends and relatives were not realistic. Most of them thought that people in America or Europe live in affluence without knowledge of what suffering is like.

They never had any evident problem in their marriage. Their efforts were directed on their survival. They did not have friends or close associate.

Fortunately they hit the "gold-mine" when their business investments paid off. A year of wealth swept off all the draughts and dregs of poverty. Their skin turned silky and their chicks became robust. They felt it would be nice to pay a visit to their roots in Africa. The trip was arranged and perfectly carried out. They were highly honored and respected on arrival. They returned to England nursing the idea of how to better the condition of their people back home in Africa. Anthony lost his father at a very tender age, his mother was his most treasured person in his life. Both of Jemima's parents were very much alive. The argument ensued on who to invite first. After a series of disagreements, they agreed to file for the two aging ladies. Jemima's Mom was to arrive first while her mother-in-law was to come six months later.

Jemima spoke with her mother in their local dialect of which Anthony had little or no under-standing. Initially he would not charge his wife and her mother for segregation and his being marginalized. He felt isolated in his own home. His greatest desire was the arrival of his mother. He chose to spend most of his time at work because his home was no longer a place of excitement to return to. Jemima paid little or no attention to the drift or disaffection that had gained ground between her and her husband. Anthony was not really a church person. His attendance was in solidarity with his wife who professed being born-again. He started growing some traits of bitterness and hatred for the Christian faith professed by his wife who tended to be insensitive and indifferent to his domestic marginalization. He decided to seek for solace in bottles of lager beer. He initially kept his 'new found partner' away from his wife.

He eventually decided to drink his beer in his house. She was surprised to come home to find her husband drinking stout beer. She screamed at him, "What is this...in this house?" "The name is stout beer, my new found companion that gives me attention. Our relationship is just three months old. I am in love with her. She speaks to me and I obey her commands when I am fully involved with her. Please go and talk to your mom and stop disturbing my conversation with my bride," he affirmed. Jemima thought she was in a trance. She rushed into her mother's room to call her attention to the development. The old lady stormed out and screamed at her son-in-law, "Anthony, what do you think you are doing?" "I am in conversation with my newfound lover. I found this conversation more reliable especially at the close of business in the past three months. Grandma, please go back to your room and continue your conversation with your 'lover-girl'," he sneered. "I guess this is demonic," his mother-in-law asserted. The word 'demonic' made him snap, "What nonsense, you came from Africa, took your daughter from me and called my solace a demonic relationship? You must be demonic too." His eruption shocked Jemima and her mother. They had never seen him so aggressive. They were very confused. Jemima threatened him, "Pastor must not hear this!" "He needs to hear these...why I found a new 'partner'? We speak same language. Please arrange a meeting with the pastor and let me know when he is ready to hear and see all these. I am in control of my new partner and I know when I want her to control me. Grandma, please go and sleep and let my wife and myself enjoy each other, this once before the end...," he retorted. Jemima was the more confused, she thought, "...who is the wife he was referring to, the bottle of beer or me?" She realized that his statements were not that of a drunken man but a man that was frustrated, in pain and fallen into the hands of the devil. She chose to be calm as she walked into the bedroom. She was very cautious of every movement of her husband. She determined to resist any proposal of the act of sex. There was a caution in her spirit not to deny him and not to be inactive or play "the-log" in bed. She had emotional pain but a psychological satisfaction and conviction that she allowed him to have his way.

She wanted to appease him after the act but he was fast asleep. She felt violated but convicted of abandoning her husband since the arrival of her mother. She spent most part of the night praying and planning how to win the love of her husband and walk her way back into his life. She slept briefly and woke up again. Her eyes were on the ceiling tiles when her husband woke up. He looked at his wife and said, "You were saved yester night, and how did you come about giving me such a good time? I had planned to beat hell into you and probably go to hell for you. I did not plan that either of us would see this morning. We would both have left your mother to call 911..." Jemima was speechless. In trepidation she burst into tears and sobbed. She said, "Thank you Holy Spirit." The mention of the Holy Spirit was like a dagger into the heart of her husband who snappily said, "Don't bring the Holy Spirit into this issue..." "But He was the one that instructed me to yield myself and do my best that I can ever give in the act. Though I had emotional and psychological pain, I felt violated if not raped but I had a measure of peace in my spirit that I was to satisfy my husband who felt offended and needed to be pacified. Therefore I yielded and gave my best. I never realized it would have been my last moment on earth," she hooted loudly.

Her husband was broken by the power of the Holy Spirit which was instigated by her obedience. He wept bitterly with his wife as he expressed his pains and frustrations. He said, "I discovered that since your mother stepped into this home she became your confidant, you both spoke your local dialect even when you had me very much around. You took counsel together, you hardly discussed any crucial issues with me. You started taking decisions unilaterally. You must realize that you declined my sexual moves and I decided never to ask you for sex until you make the move. I would not want to date any other woman in my life. I decided to suppress my pains by taking light alcohol. I got tired of hiding it from you. That was why I decided to bring it into the house. I heard a voice that told me that, should you put up any resistance on my attempt to have sex with you, I should force you and after the act, stab you repeatedly and stab myself. I was not going to kill you all because I hated but to make your mother feel the pain." He reached for the knife under the pillow. Jemima pulled back in fear with her right hand over her mouth and her left hand on her head as she shouted repeatedly, "Holy Spirit thank you...Holy Spirit thank you..." Her husband threw the knife into a corner of the bedroom, knelt down and asked her to pray for his deliverance. She quickly knelt by him, holding him to her chest as she prayed with fear and tears, thanking God and rebuking the devil and his cohorts. It was a moment of trepidation and close shave with death. Anthony wanted reconciliation and reassurance but Jemima was in great fear.

Though they reconciled their differences, so as it were, Jemima was traumatized. She spent days in fear and insecurity, she determined to quit the marriage. Her first port of call was her pastor's office. She was granted audience. She narrated her ordeal. Her pastor was very disturbed but had every reason to thank God for averting the evil. He turned to 'Sister Jemima' as she was always addressed. Looking straight into her eyes he said, "Please open your bible and read Apostle Paul's letter to the Philippines, chapter one verse six." She read, *"I am convinced and confident of this very thing, that He who has begun a good work in you will [continue to] perfect and complete it until the day of Christ Jesus [the time of His return]."* "Ok! Let me read to you a divine injunction written in Malachi 2: 16. It reads, *"For I hate divorce," says the LORD, the God of Israel, "and him who covers his garment with wrong and violence," says the LORD of hosts. "Therefore keep watch on your spirit, so that you do not deal treacherously [with your wife].""* And I would say your spouse. The error of your husband took place in his spirit. The spirit of murder came into him through bitterness, hatred, multiple offenses and alcoholism. You told me he had never been violent. Your testimony of him clearly revealed that he was a victim of the antics of the devil. You will learn to forgive him and do not allow the spirit of fear to rule your life. Please check with me, 2Tim. 1: 7. It reads, *"For God did not give us a spirit of timidity or cowardice or fear, but [He has given us a spirit] of power and of love and of sound judgment and personal discipline [abilities that result in a calm, well-balanced mind and self-control]."* He continued, "You claimed that your husband had never been violent. He requested that you should pray for him to be delivered. There is no doubt he has given you an assignment before the Lord. Are you ready to fulfill the great commission? Jesus said as the Father has sent Him so He sends you. He died for you. Are you ready to die for a soul?" He questioned. Jemima was silent for a while. She turned to her pastor and declared, "This is a very hard counsel, and you have successfully gotten me to reexamine my faith in Christ. The only way I can remain in the marriage is to reckon myself as dead..." The pastor with a smile referred to scripture, "For you died [to this world], and your [new, real] life is hidden with Christ in God." COLOSSIANS 3:3 AMP

Opening his bible to the book of Prophet Isaiah chapter 54: 16-17 he read, *"Listen carefully, I have created the smith who blows on the fire of coals And who produces a weapon for its purpose; And I have created the destroyer to inflict ruin. "No weapon that is formed against you will succeed; and every tongue that rises against you in judgment you will condemn. This [peace, righteousness, security, and triumph over opposition] is the heritage of the servants of the LORD, and this is their vindication from me," says the LORD."*

Jemima ran her eyes through the ceiling tiles as she sighed, "Pastor you are not in my shoes. I have read and quoted these verses of the scriptures times without number. It is the application that makes the difference, especially when the one quoting the scriptures is the very one to apply it. My only source of peace is to reckon myself as dead just like Esther did." She took her bible and opened it and read,

"Then Esther told them to reply to Mordecai,

"Go, gather all the Jews that are present in Susa, and observe a fast for me; do not eat or drink for three days, night or day. I and my maids also will fast in the same way. Then I will go in to [see] the king [without being summoned], which is against the law; and if I perish, I perish." So Mordecai went away and did exactly as Esther had commanded him." ESTHER 4:15-17 AMP

The pastor realized that the zeal of the counsellor in most cases may not be a match to the trauma of the counseled. He turned to his traumatized member and said, "I can feel for you. As a pastor I have had to make assessment of people on their most valued relationships or aspirations. It has always been a struggle between personal material involvements and their ultimate eternal experience. I quite agree that as at now you are in fear. Would you ever imagine or pray that you overcome the fear? I do not mean to burden you, but let me ask you a few questions:

If you choose to divorce your husband, would you remain single for the rest of your life?

Have you considered the fate of your children and the trauma of divorce?

Do you consider the impact divorce would have on your ministry? Have you considered all the souls that see you as their mentor or role-model?

Do you think heaven will accept your reasons for divorce as authentic enough?

"May I..." Jemima cut in with apology, "Sir, all I have heard you say is that I should remain in the marriage even If I have to die. You seem not to realize the reality of my experience and the gravity of the impact of the intended action of my husband on my emotions." The pastor was silent momentarily, he was about to speak but was cautioned by the Holy Spirit to allow Jemima to fully reel out her mind. She continued, "I don't think pastors are real, humane or natural. You have just told me to go and die because some people are looking up to me. They should look up to Jesus as stated in Heb: 12:2. If he kills me, my children will face a tougher trauma and challenges." She paused a little, wiping some sweats off her forehead, she continued, "Sir, I guess I have to go. I need the Lord to speak to me on this issue." The pastor watched her as she picked her bag and headed for the door. She walked out and came back to apologize to the pastor, "Sorry Sir, I didn't mean to walk out on you. I am just traumatized by the whole development." "May the Lord speak to you and pacify your spirit," the Pastor prayed in response.

Jemima felt depressed and hated by the world around her. She was alone in her car but heard a voice speaking to her almost audibly. She looked over her shoulder as if someone was at the back seat. She heard in her spirit, "Is death that dreadful? Did you know what your husband was instructed to do by the devil? Were you spoken to by man to yield to his demand for sex? Did you force him to throw away the knife? Did you force him to kneel before you for prayers? See how very soon you felt you are in the control of your life and your experience. I have promised to be with you always. If you decline my leadership and protection, take care of yourself." The voice ceased. She was terrified. She pulled up to the next available soft shoulder considered safe enough. She looked very well into every part of the car as if she was to find someone hiding. She never had such an audible communication with the Lord. She put her head on the steering wheel in meditation. A few minutes into her meditation, she was taken into the realm of the Spirit for some classified information. She was incredibly overwhelmed. She felt out of place with the angelic beings. She felt impure and repulsive to the sanity, serenity and scintillating transparency of the environment. She desired to be granted liberty to join in their spiritual ecstasy which was stupendous and exhilarating, but she could not. She was in the frenzy of her thrill when she was retracted to the terrestrial realm by a knock on the glass shield of her car. It was a police officer on patrol. She raised her head snappily in protest to the interruption of her divine encounter. Her eyes were red, her countenance was of consternation. The police officer inquired, "Are you ok mam?" She stared at him, looking straight into his eyes, she briskly looked over her shoulders and again fixed her gaze on the police officer as she lowered the glass window of the car.

"Are you ok mam, "the police officer exclaimed. With one of his hands on his gun while the other was on the windshield of the car. Jemima quickly put her two hands on the steering wheel, (A basic required level of comportment of a driver at police check-point.) She looked around with a radiant smile and said, "I am very ok, I was just having a good time in His presence." "Whose presence?" The police officer asked. "Sorry, you may not understand... I am very ok." She said affirmatively. "Can I have your driver's license please?" She handed him her driver's license. He ran her details through the system and came to give her back her driver's license. "I am happy you are ok. We have on similar instances found drivers dead or almost dead at the steering on soft shoulders by the freeways. You sounded like some religious fanatics in fantasy, who believe they are always in the presence of the Lord even on the freeways." "I am not a fanatic in fantasy but an F.B.I. In the frenzy of a taste of Heaven. Her expected intrigue with the abbreviation F.B.I. did not beat the curiosity of the police officer. He was able to understand that she was not referring to the government agency but a Christian acronym for "FIRM BELIEVER IN-CHRIST" because he himself was a Christian but would not bring it up on his duty as a police officer. With a broad smile the police officer responded, "You may get to know that you are not the only Firm Believer

In-Christ around town. Some of us are in uniform. With great excitement she screamed, "Praise the Lord." The police officer calmly said Hallelujah. He realized that he had before seen her face at a city-wide musical concert. He affirmatively said, "You are a Christian Artiste?" She was excited that her person was recognized by the police officer. She offered him a copy of her musical album. The police officer declined with a smile as he said, "Not when I am on duty. Please drive safely." They parted.

Jemima could not get over her experience. She determined to forgive her husband and believe he was genuinely repentant and in the process of total deliverance from the control of the devil. She returned home with excitement. Determined to treat her husband with her utmost attention and affection. She went straight into the kitchen. Made one of the best dinners she could ever dream of. She gave her husband a very unusual welcome and informed him that the table was set for dinner just a few minutes before his arrival. Her mother declined joining them at the table. She decided to ignore her mom who had tried to put her under pressure since she did not give her the usual attention at the expense of her husband and a detriment to their marital relationship. She determined to win the mind of her husband at all cost. She posed as a new lover. Her husband could hardly believe his experience. He was happy but troubled by the exceptional affection, submission, care and attention. After about two weeks into the unusual honeymoon, he invited his wife for a special bedroom discussion. "My dear, I am compelled to call this meeting because I am excited, impressed and also afraid. I cannot understand what exactly is going on. Something strange must have happened. If your care is not a prelude to my death, it must be the beginning of my taste of heaven on earth."

With a broad smile, she hugged him and gave him a kiss. She began the narratives of her discussion with the pastor and the pastor's prayer that preceded her spiritual encounter. She claimed that words cannot describe her encounter in the realm of the spirit. She tried to describe the splendor of heaven with no adequate vocabulary. Looking straight into the eyes of her husband she said, "You are the crown of my head to whom I determine to express my love of heaven so that I do not miss out on my experience." He was in tears as he said, "I did not expect this, and neither do I deserve it from you. I was scared of you when you started all you did to me in the past two weeks. I have never ever felt convicted of sin as much as I felt for your acceptance of my person after I had scared life out of you." She joined him in the 'tear-flow'. They wept and ended up praying together. It was a wonderful experience that bonded them together afresh. Her husband held her to his chest as he said, "I must confess, today you won my heart for Christ. I have followed you to church all this while to please you and keep our relationship. I joined the church because of you. I love your voice and your songs. When you neglected me for your mom, I cannot explain where the hatred came from. The same voice of yours became an irritant to my ears. I felt like keeping your company as usual after you prayed for me on that demonic sacrilegious night. But now I have determined to give my life to Jesus and reciprocate his love for me through you. Your Christian virtues won my heart for the Lord." He knelt down and continued, "I have been old enough in the church to know all the Christian rites and rituals but now, not in rituals, please lead me to Christ." With sobs and prayers he prayed the sinner's prayer as dictated by his wife. His amen at the end of the prayer was thunderous.

Since Jemima's mom did not get the usual attention from her daughter, she determined to make her feel sorry for her action. She declined many of her regular domestic chores. Her action was more offensive to her daughter than her son-in-law. Based on agreement between Jemima and her husband Anthony's mother was invited. It was their belief that the two parents would relate freely and spend time together to afford a good relationship and rapport with the children. The filing was done in no time. Grandma Eliot was granted access into the country. On arrival she was adequately informed and given an induction program of the setting of things in the family. Grandma Eliot enjoyed cooking and was never stressed with the domestic chores. She came in at a very crucial moment because Grandma Thompson declined most of her domestic assistance. There was no doubt that grandma Eliot was a better cook. She was doing great but with every carefulness. She would not want to take over the kitchen because she noticed that grandma Thompson had displayed some traits of jealousy over the control of the kitchen. She decided to pull back from cooking and to assist in taking good care of the children.

Jemima could not handle the cold-war set in motion against her and her mother-in-law. The entire home was a war front laced with 'land mines.' Jemima suggested that her mother should return to her home country, a proposal that was vehemently declined by her mother. Grandma Thompson called everyone that she could talk to, to caution her daughter to disengage herself on what she called the plot of Anthony and his mother. The matter became very dirty. Grandma Eliot was very grieved about the entire issue. She called her son and her daughter-in-law to a meeting. She suggested that she should be allowed to return to her home country in order to afford peace in the family. The idea did not go well with Anthony but he was of the opinion that he would not object to the proposal if that would afford them the desired peace. Jemima was of a different opinion. She claimed her mother should be compelled to return to Africa because she had declined in her domestic assistance to the family. Anthony did not want to agree with his wife's proposal. He claimed it would paint a bad image of his mother. Unknown to them all, grandma Thompson who was assumed to be asleep was fully awake and was listening with her ears glued to the wall. Though she did not hear a sizable part of the discussion, she did not miss out on the contention between her daughter and her son-in-law on the issue of who should return to Africa. She was very enraged. She opened the door on them and strongly charged at her daughter. She affirmatively said they both must be compelled to return to Africa if she had to go. Jemima was very angry. She advised her mother to go back to her room, asserting that she was the cause of the entire disruption. A charge her mother unequivocally rebutted. She railed on her a set of denunciations that could make one feel she was not her biological mother. Then she finally made a reference to the almost attempted murder issue which her daughter shared with her in confidence. She warned her not to ever cry to her when the knife is placed on her throat. To Jemima it was a height of betrayal. She dropped her head and was sobbing profusely. Anthony went straight to his wife and lifted her up with words of encouragement and assurance that he is now a child of God and that no demonic insinuation would ever win him over. His mother-in-law shouted at him, "Is it now that you want to call me the one with demonic insinuation? Let us wait and see." She turned to Anthony's mother who was oblivious of the issue of attempted murder. She asked her, "Didn't your son tell you he was about to kill my daughter?" Jemima was very devastated. She pulled the hand of her husband and they both went into their bedroom. She subbed profusely as she apologized to her husband over the almost forgotten issue of the past. She confessed that she confided in her mother and her pastor on the issue. Anthony claimed not to take any offense on the divulged information. He said, "The trust and responsibility rest on me to prove every skeptic wrong. I have determined not to assume that the whole world will not get to know something about my past. I was just not bold enough to share it openly. However from today I will be willing to share it on the television. That will be the evidence of my victory." His wife looked at him in amazement and concluded in her heart that he was now truly a child of God. She knelt before him and pled for forgiveness. She promised henceforth never to share her deepest pain in marriage with anyone without his knowledge.

Anthony and his wife had a big lump to swallow. She was fed up with her mother while he was struggling with winning the mind of his mother-in-law and forging reconciliation between the three women in the house. Jemima seemed to be in good rapport with her mother-in-law, a development that incurred the displeasure of her mother. Anthony was not accepted by his mother-in-law. His liberty and freedom of expression of his love towards his mother was viewed by his mother-in-law as a gang-up for evil plotting or rebellion. Anthony's mother was in a fix. She felt like going back to her husband back in Africa. The house became a tense environment for them all. He was of the opinion that his mother should return to her business in Africa. The dialogue between him and his wife ended in a contention. Jemima accused her husband of cowardice, she could not understand why he could not agree with her that her mother should be asked to return to Africa. According to her, the purpose of inviting her had been defeated. Anthony claimed that all the efforts and money spent on his mother-in-law's green card would go down the drain. His greatest fear was the fact that many of his in-laws would blackmail his mother as the person responsible for the conflict between his wife and her mother. Anthony determined to absorb any unpleasant comment or statement in connection with all the developments. He had the understanding that the devil was just doing his worst to disrupt the peace of his family. He turned to his wife and jokingly said, "I accept my cowardice while I salute your bravery to face the storms. Just make sure that your sail is strong enough to use the storm to move in the right direction." She smiled and reaffirmed that she was moving in the right direction. Her husband gently whispered, "Please, listen to me, let us move in my own direction. I guess my idea is better this time around." She turned around and looked straight into her husband's eyes with the statement, "Do not allow affliction to rise the second time." Anthony thought over his wife's statement and consented. He knew he would be counted responsible for every negative development should things go wrong. "Are you ready to bell the cat?" He asked his wife. "I know you do not have the courage to face my Mom. I am her daughter, I will convey our decisions on the ongoing issues. She cannot disown me, she will have no choice but to live with the consequences of her actions." The final agreement was that the two grandmas would have to return to their respective homes. It was not a big issue with Anthony's mother but a great setback for Jemima's mom. A flight ticket was bought for the return of Jemima's mom. Mrs. Elliott's return ticket was still valid. They both returned to their respective homes. There was no doubt that the close and extended families were wounded and strained. Jemima determined to focus on her nucleus family and stood against any external interference or infiltration. Though she seemed to be winning, she had inner pressure that she was not strong enough to conquer. She turned to her husband for agreement that they seek the counsel of their pastor on the consequences of what she thought was a victory.

They met with the pastor the same day they requested for the meeting. The pastor could not afford to delay his attention for the Elliot family due to the previous development. The administrative secretary was instructed by the pastor to allow the Elliots to come straight into his office on arrival.

They were very prompt on keeping to time. The pastor received them with enthusiasm. Jemima led the talking. She expressed her pains on the experience she had with her mother and the influence she had on her marriage. She felt grieved by the pain of the strain between her and her mother. She claimed to have made a comparison of the life and disposition of her mother and her mother-in-law. The comment was a boost to her husband's ego. He felt proud of his mother's personal comportment, composure and maturity in the course of the matrimonial contentions. The pastor was impressed by the agreements between the couple. He counseled, "I am happy for you both on the victory over the invasion of the devil against your family. I may not be able to lay my hands firmly on the source of your victory but I am very sure that there is no doubt that the Holy Spirit must have played a vital role in it all. You have successfully waded through the stream that drowned many marriages by sending the couples into perpetual hatred for each other. One thing that I need to encourage you to do is to allow the spirit of Christ to rule your hearts. Please forgive each other completely and forgive your parents or in-laws that have offended or would still offend you." She looked in the direction of her husband as if she was asking for assistance on how to handle the suggestion of the pastor. The pastor said to her, "It is good that the core of the contention is between you and your mother. Please forgive her and reach out to her in love, however do your best to retain your faithfulness and allegiance to your husband. By now you both must have understood the importance of *'The exchange of parents'* in marital relationship." They both looked at each other. Jemima raised her hands for the pastor's approval for her to ask a question.

She was granted the right, "Sir, what should a marriage partner do when his or her in-law do not want to accept him or her." The pastor responded, "Love." Anthony cautiously cut in, "I have shown love to my mother-in-law, all to no avail." The pastor responded, *"Love, love love, "* As he reached for his bible. He read 1Corinthians 13: 3-8

"If I give all my possessions to feed the poor, and if I surrender my body to be burned, but do not have love, it does me no good at all. Love endures with patience and serenity, love is kind and thoughtful, and is not jealous or envious; love does not brag and is not proud or arrogant. It is not rude; it is not self-seeking, it is not provoked [nor overly sensitive and easily angered]; it does not take into account a wrong endured. It does not rejoice at injustice, but rejoices with the truth [when right and truth prevail]. Love bears all things [regardless of what comes], believes all things [looking for the best in each one], hopes all things [remaining steadfast during difficult times], and endures all things [without weakening]. Love never fails [it never fades nor ends]. But as for prophecies, they will pass away; as for tongues, they will cease; as for the gift of special knowledge, it will pass away." 1 COR. 13:3-8 AMP

Anthony took a deep breath and said, "I guess I have a long way to go." With a smile the pastor responded, "We all have a long way to go. We need the Holy Spirit to guide us to act right when we get caught in the web of challenges that test our measure of love." Jemima put her hand on her husband's shoulder, to get his attention as she said, "I know you have promised to win the love of my mom so that we may have peace in our home. May I advise you not to stress yourself if she is persistently resistant. I have spoken to her about it but to no avail." "What was her response?" Anthony asked. "I do not have to tell you, you saw it already, just remain persistent and resilient as the Bible requires of you." She retorted. Her husband was a little disturbed but summoned courage to respond with pleasant words as he said, "I surely will be persistent and resilient as you advised. I promise you she will have no choice but to accept me as her only son-in-law. I have never perceived or understood the text read by the pastor in the perspective at which I got it today. I am determined to make it work for me." "I am anxious to listen to your testimony soonest." She chipped in, "I will make sure that you are not a false prophet. I will surely have a good testimony." He responded. "I pray you prove the imagination of your wife wrong," the pastor added. Everyone smiled. "You both seem to have gotten a good understanding of "Parental-exchange," the pastor asserted. With a stern look on his face, he turned to Jemima and said, "You will need to be cautious of your attitude towards your mother, realize that in practical criticism, you see first in others what you hate in yourself. Be careful that you do not do the same to your prospective son-in-law." "I may have a little trait of my mother, but I am more of my father in terms of my temperamental disposition. Please don't compare me with my mother." The pastor sensed the offense in her voice. "I am sorry, but you will always be her daughter, he added. Anthony was quiet as he would not want to confirm the assertions of the pastor. Jemima stared at her husband and snapped, "Your silence means consent. Am I like my mother?" With a smile her husband responded, You are a unique personality, the daughter of Mr. and Mrs. Thompson." The pastor and Anthony smiled but Jemima was not pleased with her husband's response. He turned in her direction and said, "From Pastor's teaching, from now she is my mother, I will surely do my best to change your impression of her." "I wish you both the best," she responded. The pastor prayed with them and they took their leave.

Grandma Thompson was going to be sixty years old. Anthony had liaised with the siblings of his wife on the celebration without her knowledge. He actually told them to keep the plan a secret and play indifferent should their mother talk about it. When she eventually mentioned her desires to her children, their response was that they did not have any money to fund the projected expenses. They advised her to contact their sister or her son-in-law in England. A line of action that she declined to pursue. She resolved to mark her sixtieth birthday with an in-house get-together. The entire plan was top secret. Jemima suspected that her husband was on a regular phone call to Africa but would not want to probe into his intentions. Anthony had already shipped a befitting car for the sixtieth birthday celebration. He made a secret arrangement with her boss at her job to give her two weeks off work towards the celebration. He already bought the flight tickets for them both. A couple of days to their travel date he called his wife to a bedroom talk. He said, "I am sure you know that 'my Mom' would be sixty years old in four days from now and I have to be there." "To be where?" She snarled at her husband. "Don't you think it right for me to be there?" He questioned. "Who is funding the celebration?" "You and my other mother. " He pulled out the travel documents and the documents of the car that had been made ready back in Africa. She flared up, "How do you expect me to travel in two days' time? I cannot afford to lose my job for any celebration. My boss requires at least a month notice for me to be granted such a leave of absence." With a smile, her husband said, "That is already taken care of." He showed her the letter from her boss which expressly granted her the leave of absence commencing from the very date of the proposed trip. She disdained him and said, "You cannot do this to me, how can you plan my life and movement without my knowledge. I already have a plan for the weekend. I am not going to any celebration." "Yes, you are not going to any celebration but 'my Mom's' 60th Birthday party, at least her blood runs in your veins, though you claim to be a complete departure from her temperamental disposition. By this we shall know if you yield." With a small smiles she retorted, "I guess you planned a blackmail which will not happen..." "I am happy you will prove me wrong," her husband responded. They embraced each other as he handed over to her an envelope and said, "Here is a thousand Pounds for your shopping." Her face became very radiant. She gave him a kiss as she snappily said, "Oh noooo! I am supposed to lead the praise worship in church this coming Sunday..." "The Pastor knows you are traveling and has notified the choirmaster." "Whoa-oooo. All these plans went behind me. I am happy you are now a good Christian brother and a wonderful husband. You would have been a terrible coup-planner. You see why it is dangerous to have a sinner spouse," she asserted. With broad smiles they kissed. "I'd better start packing my luggage as you have planned," she concluded.

The trip was a good one, the celebration was wonderful. Grandma Thompson was beaten hollow. She was speechless. She opened her mouth agape with incredulity when the beautiful car was driven to the center of the hall and she was handed the key. She embraced her son-in-law for the very first time as she said, "I never would imagine you will do this for me. I had never wanted you to marry my daughter, I did all I could to destroy your relationship but you have won my heart through love." She burst into tears. Anthony wiped her face with the fringe of his flowing gown. It was a very emotional moment for them both. Jemima watched with amazement. She went close and whispered into her husband's ear, "You made it. You kept your word and you won her heart.Mrs. Elliot was present. The new found love for Anthony by her mother-in-law was extended to his surviving parent. It was the true beginning of a family union that enhanced their conjugal relationship.

CHAPTER NINE

"MARRIAGE BY ASSOCIATION"

Janet Hughes was attracted to Janet Hedges at their first day of their orientation in college. Their names were mistaken for each other. They bonded so much that they were suspected by their colleagues to be lesbians. At a point they chose to dress alike. They both were beautiful and charming, their close relationship fenced them off many of the young prospective suitors. It was a good advantage for them because it afforded them the pleasure of concentrating on their studies. In their final year they both felt it was necessary for them to open themselves to the fancy of prospective suitors. Janet Hughes introduced her brother to her friend, a proposal that was tainted by passion, fantasy and exuberance rather than personal conviction. The relationship started with nuptial effervescence. Eric Hughes was anxious to crown his new found love with holy wedlock. The wedding was contracted. Everything went on well until there was a misunderstanding between Eric and his wife on the issue of expected support for his in-law and the siblings of his wife. He discovered that his wife had been sending money to her parents without his knowledge. Though Janet sent money to her parents, she always told her parents that the money was sent by her husband. The cat was let out of the bag when her parents called her husband to thank him for all the money he had purportedly sent to them. Eric received the appreciation without giving his in-laws the slightest reason to suspect his surprise and shock. The contention escalated. Mrs. Janet Hughes notified his friend about the development. The interference of Miss Janet Hughes did not win the approval of her fiancée, Derrick Hogan. She was in opposition of her brother's reaction to what she called the good gesture of her friend because the money was sent on his behalf. Derrick was crossed with his fiancé. He claimed Mrs. Janet Hughes was high handed on the issue. Eric was very offended, he felt his sister and her friend had ganged up against him. He was determined to fence his sister off the relationship between him and his wife. Along the line, the contention filtered to the hearing of both parents who shared different opinions on the development. The relationship between both families was very strained. Eric felt he could not trust his wife. His wife felt he was insensitive to the plight of her parents who got into trouble in their business and had to file for bankruptcy. She saw her husband as an ingrate, who quickly forgot all that her parents spent for the success of their wedding. The home front was more dangerous than the war front. Eric and his wife lived as if they were roommates. Verbal communication was reduced to the bare minimum. They wrote notes to each other for notification of their movements and lines of action. The situation at home had less effect on Eric a phlegmatic melancholic who used the development as an opportunity to enjoy his solitude. He had always been more productive when he had less interaction with anybody. The setting of things in the family was detrimental to his wife, a choleric sanguine. She could not hold it in any longer. She decided to notify their Pastor of the ongoing rift in her marriage. An appointment was fixed for Eric and Janet Hughes to meet with the pastor on a day when it was very unlikely for anybody to be around the church office. This was at the request of Janet. She wouldn't want anyone to suspect that there was any rift in her marriage. The pastor referred them to his teachings on "PARENTAL-EXCHANGE." He questioned whether they read his book, "Marriage manual for new couples". Popularly referred to as, "NewCouples'M2." They felt ashamed of themselves because they never created time to read it. The pastor attributed their challenges to a lack of knowledge. He opened his bible to Hosea 4: 6 and gave it to Eric to read. He read,

"My people are destroyed for lack of knowledge [of My law, where I reveal My will]. Because you [the priestly nation] have rejected knowledge, I will also reject you from being My priest. Since you have forgotten the law of your God, I will also forget your children."

The pastor flipped the pages of the Bible to the book of Prophet Jeremiah 33:3. He handed it to Janet to read.

She read,

"'Call to Me and I will answer you, and tell you [and even show you] great and mighty things, [things which have been confined and hidden], which you do not know and understand and cannot distinguish.'"

Looking at them both, he emphatically told them that they were the architect of their present challenges because they had not created time to study their marriage manual, the Holy Bible and associated publications. He advised them to forgive each other and take a good step of faith to read the Bible especially on those chapters that hinged on relationships. According to the Pastor, "Marriage is the only institution that gives you your certificate on admission, with the expectation that you will learn to earn the benefits attached to the certificate." Eric and his beautiful wife looked at each other's eyes as if to ask the question, "Are you ready to learn?" They both promised the Pastor that they would read the recommended books and their Bible. It was time to leave the Pastor's office. The Pastor charged them to make sure that the Holy Spirit is granted permanent residency in their home. He should be the chairperson at every discussion and deliberation. Finally he cautioned, "Please do your best possible to relegate every third party into oblivion in your relationship if you want to have wonderful experience in your marriage." Eric and Janet left the pastor's office with a rekindled nuptial-fire. At the door, Eric handed to the Pastor an envelope in appreciation of his dedication to the ministry. The Pastor said some prophetic prayers as they walked along the corridor. A resounding amen from the couple rented the air.

Eric had a task of how to walk his way back into the hearts of his parent-in-laws. He decided to call them on the phone very often before a proposed visit. He sent them a letter of appreciation and concern for their current financial challenges after the bankruptcy. He explained himself as being principled and not antagonistic of the gesture of his wife on the remittances. He was easily accepted by his father-in-law, but Mrs. Hedges still held him guilty of indifference and lack of appreciation of the reputation that his wife tried to build of him in their hearts. Mr. and Mrs. Hedges were at variance in their perception of the good intention of their daughter. The argument got so bad that Mrs. Hedges felt very crossed, especially in response to her husband's statement, "Any money spent outside of the regulated expenses of the family is a stolen fund." He felt his wife was being sentimental and partisan of feminism. She asserted that his statement insinuated that their daughter was adjudged a thief. Therefore he should withdraw the statement and apologize. Her husband was adamant. He claimed he owed no one any apology for a valid statement. They both went to bed without a word of prayer or their usual goodnight kiss.

The break of the morning was made good by Mr. Hedges. He rolled over to his wife's side of the bed and put his lips to hers as he said, "Good morning, please accept the kisses I owed and please accept my apology for the hurt of yesterday." His wife was impressed. She appreciated him for his magnanimity. She said, "Yes I took serious offense over the subject of our discussions yesterday night. I later realized, I have allowed the issue of third party to infringe on our relationship. I am equally very sorry for being too personal on the issue." Her husband responded with deep affection that resulted into 'early-morning-shower-of-blessings.'

The relationship between Derrick Hogan and Janet Hughes was to be consummated but the overall arrangement did not win the approval of Pa. Hughes. There was a family meeting on what needed to be done and what should not be allowed. The parents of Derrick Hogan would not compromise their ground on the issue of alcohol. They unequivocally undauntedly refused to include the requested six bottles of Gin in the list of the items demanded as part of the bride price. Their reason was based on their profession of faith. Pa. Hughes believed that Jesus turned water into wine, therefore there would be no reason for a professing Christian to abstain completely from anything that contains alcohol. He claimed even the wedding cakes have a percentage of alcohol. The two families could not reach a compromise until the final days. It was finally proposed that the six bottles of Gin be excluded from the bridal list while the bridal price be increased. At this juncture, Pa. Hughes decided to 'soft-pedal' on the issue as his daughter felt he was blackmailing the family. She pleaded with tears such that her father could not resist. Though Pa. Hughes consented, he held it in his heart against his prospective In-laws. The wedding was a beautiful ceremony. It was the talk of the town in the Christian community. Not many knew about the demand for alcohol by Grandpa Hughes but the news invariably spread around town. It did not put the family in a good light amongst the Brethren. The spread of the bad impression was believed by the Hughes household to be the handiwork of the Hogan family.

Few weeks after the very successful wedding ceremony, Janet and Derrick Hogan decided to visit the Granny Hughes. They were well received but unfortunately the issue of alcohol was revisited. The argument did not end on a good note. Pa. Hughes was very intolerant of his son-in-law and his daughter who solidly stood in solidarity with her husband. The parting was not pleasant. The young couple returned to their home with the impression that they were not welcome in the Hughes family. When the news of the conflict got to Mrs. Janet Hughes née Hedges, it took a different turn as they were already wrongly informed that the Hogans were bent on character assassination against the Hughes family. Mrs. Janet Hogan felt betrayed by her friend to have believed that members of her husband's family were out to destroy the Hughes family to which the two Janets belonged by birth and marriage respectively. Janet Hogan was loud, strenuous and 'mean' when she said she was going to confront her father on the issue. Her brother felt she was unruly to have directly or indirectly adjudged their father as guilty of the spread of wrong information of intended blackmail against the Hogan family. He warned her to be quiet otherwise he would teach her a lesson on how to speak about her parents. His comment and emotional outburst was very offensive to Janet's husband, Mr. Derrick Hogan. Though he did not utter a word but his facial expression said it all. All this happened at the very first visit of Janet and Eric Hughes to the new home of Janet and Derrick Hogan. They were about to part when Derrick said to Mr. Eric Hughes, "Congratulations that you did not abuse or assault my wife... you would have known that she is now the wife of a one-time bouncer. She ceases to be that little girl that you tossed around in your family home." Janet the wife of Eric felt that was a slap on the face of her husband who happened to be older and more-so a brother-in-law to Derrick. The development actually strained the relationship between the two Janets. Mrs. Janet Hogan felt grossly offended that her friend was in the support of her big-brother who was about to beat her up in her husband's house. The two families parted on a very bad note.

God has always been faithful, the family of Eric and Janet Hughes was blessed with a baby boy. The naming ceremony was fixed to take place in the church hall. The choice of venue made things a little easier for Derrick Hogan who had vowed not to visit the Hughes family until he was formally invited, not on the basis of ceremonies or coincidences. He would not want to attend the naming ceremony but for the level of relationship between him and his wife who could not afford to be absent. As they drove towards the church hall, Janet appealed to her husband to please make sure he went to greet her parents wherever they were seated. With a tincture of a smile gliding across his face he replied, "They are my in-laws and your very precious parents. I am fully persuaded to do whatever is required of me to let them know I have a good respect for them. Janet sighed as she said, "Thank you my dear." Derrick responded with a smile, "I can see the hands of the devil in all these negative developments. It is our duty and responsibility to make sure that the devil fails." Looking at him straight in his eyes she questioned, "Will you relate freely with my brother also?" "O yes. At least I have successfully registered in his mind that he needs to treat you with some level of dignity and respect now that you are a married woman." "I trust you will keep your word to make me find fulfillment and get reconnected to my parents and siblings," she said. Her husband pulled her a little closer as they walked the entrance of the hall and whispered to her ear, "I have watched your demeanor since we talked about this naming ceremony. I knew your heart desire and I have purpose in my heart to make you happy especially as you are carrying our baby or babies. I guess it is a good occasion to inform our parents that the Lord has blessed our efforts in "biological evangelism" "They both stepped into the hall with very broad smiles and laughter. It couldn't have been a coincidence but a divine orchestration that they ran into Eric as they stepped into the hall. Derrick quickly surged forward and grabbed his hand from the rear with a radiant smile and embrace which was perfectly reciprocated. Janet stood by with a radiant smile as she respectfully greeted her brother who pulled her close with a peck on the chick as he fondly addressed her as, "JJ." The setting of things really diffused all the fears of Janet Hogan.

The naming ceremony was well attended and perfectly conducted with evident good time management. Photographs were taken in order as arranged. The two Janets and Grandma Janet Hughes happily took a picture together, an action that was described as Janets' conference by Eric Hughes. Grandpa Hughes said in jealousy, "I guess we the husbands of Janets should take our own group photograph too". It was a very animating, unifying and fulfilling action taking the group photograph.

Derrick called his in-laws aside and humbly informed them that their daughter was pregnant. Janet walking towards her parents in style was greeted by her mother with this song,

"You are welcome in the name of the Lord...2ce.

We can see all over you, the glory of the Lord...,

You are welcome in the name of the Lord..."

Pa Hughes cut in to say, "The 'bedroom evangelist' just told us you won a soul or more to the glory of the Lord..."

"O yes Mom and Dad. We are yet to confirm the full span of his evangelistic strength," Janet responded. It was all laughter and smiles.

The meeting was the best ever since the two Janets got married.

When they were in a lighter mood, Janet Hogan née Hughes turned to her longtime friend and said, "Now that you are Mrs. Hughes, you need to treat me with a measure of respect and do your best to sustain my approval of you by making sure you take good care of me as the younger sister of your husband. Always remember that In-laws are to be respected." With a good smile that turned into loud laughter Mrs. Janet Hughes responded, "I guess I need to take you through a Bible study. She reached into her bag and brought out her Bible. She read from Matthew 19: 4-6:

"'Jesus replied, "Have you never read that He who created them from the beginning MADE THEM MALE AND FEMALE, and said, 'FOR THIS REASON A MAN SHALL LEAVE HIS FATHER AND MOTHER AND SHALL BE JOINED INSEPARABLY TO HIS WIFE, AND THE TWO SHALL BECOME ONE FLESH '? So they are no longer two, but one flesh. Therefore, what God has joined together, let no one separate."...If you got it right, you are to treat me as your big-sister because I am now part of your BIG-BROTHER. If you don't, I will return to my parents. Remember how my parents wept when I chose to wed your brother. They really missed me. I am sure that has been the reason why you all take good care of me, else I will run back to my parents. I am sure you have not forgotten my then beautiful room of those days. It is still there.'"* Everybody laughed.

Grandpa Hughes rounded-off the discussion with this statement, "I am happy for you both. May the Lord sustain your relationship and strengthen the bond of your friendship. You both have your good points and claim to good respect from each other. Your friendship will be sustained by mutual respect." It was a nice meeting that strengthened the bond between the four families. Derrick Hogan was overjoyed by the reconciliation. He called his parents who could not attend the naming ceremony due to multiple engagements and distance. They were equally impressed and very happy with the reconciliation.

Time is the most essential commodity that poses the greatest challenge to humanity. The greatest ambition of man is the desire to conquer time. Good time management is one of the great determinants of human success and accomplishments. It is interesting how time flies. The first child of Janet Hughes, Sylvester was to graduate from high school. He was in the same grade with Tammy the son of Janet Hogan because he was born premature at twenty eight weeks. He grew up a normal child. He was always taunted with the word, "Ambishoow" an expression that suggested that he is ambitious and in a hurry to come into the world. His level of intelligence was far above that of his colleagues. Both children were to graduate on the same day but at different locations. The popular opinion was for them to merge the graduation celebration party but Grandpa Hughes would not allow the idea to work. Janet Hughes could not disclose the reason why the party could not be merged. When she came under serious pressure from her friend, she had no choice but to tell her that it was due to the objection of Grandpa Hughes. The matter stirred a lot of conflict in the family. Janet Hogan confronted her father on the issue. He claimed he was not responsible for the stoppage of the merger. Janet Hughes claimed that was her perception of his insinuations when the move was made. Janet Hogan charged her friend for indicting her father. The matter went out of hand. It became a big rift that almost ruined the relationship between the Janets. At a point the strained relationship became obvious to the siblings and children. Grandma Hogan was very disappointed in Grandpa Hughes. In her opinion, Grandpa Hughes was responsible for all the disruptions. The relationships in both close and extended family were badly strained.

Janet Hughes became skeptical of her parent in-laws and the siblings of her husband. She believed that Grandpa Hughes had schooled them all against her. In her opinion, Grandma was also in support of her husband. She became a victim of paranoia. She became suspicious of every action, reaction or inactions of her In-laws without any ground or evidence to justify her convictions. Her perceptions affected the relationship between her and her husband Eric. There was no doubt that Eric had a great love and emotional attachment to his mother. His wife was quite aware of this fact, she played it safe whenever she threw her tantrums.

When Janet Hughes became pregnant of her second child, she was not anxious to inform her parent-in-laws that anything was going on. She was eight months pregnant when her husband informed his mother that his wife would be delivered of another baby in the next few weeks. His mother took offense against him and his wife. She was very crossed with her daughter-in-law. Eric Hughes informed his wife about the reaction of his parents but she couldn't care less. She was successfully delivered of the baby at a time that her mother-in-law was out of the country. Her husband was out of state and her friend Janet was undergoing training in a fairly distant city from their residence. It was obviously difficult if not impossible for most of her in-laws to pay her a visit while she was in the hospital before and after delivery. She took very great offense against her in-laws including her soul mate friend. Her mother was the only parent that stayed with her towards the end of the pregnancy and delivery, especially because her husband had to be on his new job out of town. Her husband flew in for the naming ceremony. At the naming ceremony she gently charged at her father-in-law that he did not come to see her since she was delivered of the baby. Her expression was very indicting, a probe of his reason for showing up late. Her father-in-law tendered an unreserved apology for his inability to visit her, a development he attributed to overwhelming multiple involvements. He took her enigmatic smile as an acceptance of his apology. Pictures were taken. The naming ceremony was a very successful occasion.

Grandma Hughes successfully returned from her trip. She sent a message to her daughter-in-law that she was going to come to her residence to visit the almost two week old grandchild. She notified her of the date and time of her proposed visit. Janet deliberately went out with her baby to deny her mother-in-law the privilege or access to her grandchild. Grandma Hughes met Grandma Hedges in the house. She was unequivocally informed by her co-grandma that Janet went out to avoid her access to the baby. Grandma Hughes was very offended. She expressed her pains to her co-grandma so that her daughter-in-law would be adequately informed on her return home. Grandma Hughes departed in frustration. She narrated her experience to her son over the phone. He took offense but could not express his pains because information had it that his wife may be passing through a phase of postnatal depression. The incident caused additional strain to the fragile relationship between the two families. Grandma Hughes returned home and narrated her ordeal to her husband. She called her daughter to inform her of her experience and the humiliation she suffered in the hands of her daughter-in-law. Janet could not believe the narratives of her mother. She called her friend to hear her side of the story. She was shocked when her friend (Mrs. Hughes) responded, "Why should she come to see the baby, was she not aware of my prospective delivery before she travelled?" Her response was very offensive to her soul mate friend who politely told her she would call back later. She was very troubled. She called her elder brother to intimate him with the state of things in the family. Her brother made a passionate appeal to her that she should view her friend's response as a consequence of postnatal depression. The mention of postnatal depression made a very serious impact on Janet Hogan and gave her a great concern. She decided to head straight to the home of her friend. The meeting was an unpleasant one. Mrs. Janet Hughes was very rude and unfriendly. She claimed not to have any postnatal depression as most members of the close and extended family were made to believe. She narrated her plights and her reasons for becoming very aggressive and offensive against almost all her in-laws. She charged her friend for negligence and abandonment. She also claimed that her in-laws were responsible for every rift between her and her husband and that her friend, Mrs. Janet Hogan was the principal culprit. Janet was very upset. She however promised her she would want to believe that she was not in the right frame of mind. The assertion actually infuriated Mrs. Janet Hughes. She cursed her friend out. It almost resulted into a brawl but for the intervention of Mrs. Hedges who had almost become a permanent resident in her daughter's home. Janet Hogan née Hughes left the place in a rage. She determined never to visit her brother's family again. It was not possible for Mrs. Hughes to see her grandchild before she made her next trip out of state. She was seriously pained. In her personal appraisal of the entire issue, she could not advance any valid reason why her daughter-in-law should treat her that bad.

Janet Hughes was restless, her nemesis had caught up with her. She never had the boldness to call her mother-in-law to apologize or make excuses for her action. She decided to seek counsel from her pastor on the issue. She narrated the whole story to the pastor. She embellished it such that she could win the sympathy of the pastor. However the pastor was able to discern what was wrong. He blamed Janet for her very rude action. He told her that every human action is a very fertile seed that in most cases germinates, grows and yields its fruits in multiple consequences. Janet was broken. She wept and promised the pastor that she would call her mother-in-law to tender her unreserved apology. As she walked out of the pastor's office her phone rang, it was her mother-in-law. She did not have the courage to pick the call. She went back to the pastor. She appealed that the pastor should stand with her to appease her mother-in-law as she was about to return her call. The pastor assured her of his readiness to plead her cause. She dialed the number, her mother-in-law responded, "Hello my daughter! How are you, hope everything is very well with you. I called just to check on you." The pastor heard the statement of Grandma Hughes, because the phone was on speaker. The pastor adjudged the mother-in-law as very righteous and peace seeking. He chose to listen more to the trend of the conversations so as to know where and when he could actually come into the discussion. Janet tendered her apologies which were well received. Janet went further as she said, "Grandma, do you also believe that I had postnatal depression? Did you attribute my action to any medical condition? Do you think something is wrong with me?" "You are very ok right now, I believe your offense against me may be due to a challenging situation that you were not able to handle successfully. As you have refuted your husband's attribution of all your negative reactions to postnatal depression, so may it forever remain in the mighty name of Jesus. May you never have any postnatal depression. The fact is that in most cases the one depressed may not be able to agree to the defect. I am happy you are very alright." Janet was silent for a while before she regained herself. She signaled to the pastor to come into the discussion. The pastor declined and advised her to sincerely again apologize to her mother-in-law. Instead of apologizing, she informed her mother-in-law that she had come to report herself to the pastor on the account of her action against her. Her and her pastor expected an offended response. "I now agree with you that you did not have postnatal depression. I have already forgiven you of your very painful action which was your reaction to a development that was beyond my reasonable control. Please put behind you any offense you took against everyone that did not come to see you before or after you were delivered of the baby." With a tincture of laughter she added, "It was good that most of us attributed your reactions to a suspected postnatal depression. Postnatal...prenatal or "post-postnatal", I am happy you are fine. You are forgiven." At this juncture, the pastor cut in to appreciate the maturity and magnanimity of Grandma Hughes. It was a good moment of reconciliation. "So when are you bringing the baby to me at least to see her for the very first time?" "I am very ready right now if you send the flight ticket." Janet humorously responded. The pastor cut in and said, "Thank God for technology, you can watch the baby on the screen of your phone if the mother makes a video call on WhatsApp." "That is not like seeing the baby, anyways, half-bread is better than none," Grandma responded. They all laughed. The pastor made a sign to Janet that she should tell her mother-in-law that she would call back right now to let her have a view of the baby. She did. It was very animating and unifying. Janet could not express her joy well enough. She thanked her mother-in-law for receiving her back into her heart. She was very appreciative of the counsel and support of the pastor. She called her husband right there in the pastor's office to appreciate the pastor for the reconciliation. Mr. Eric Hughes was very happy to speak to the pastor. He expressed his heartfelt appreciation.

After the business of the day, Eric called his wife to share with her the trauma and ordeal he had passed through on his job since the conflicts ensued. He told his wife that he had received two cautionary notes and queries from his boss for some unexpected costly mistakes. She assured him that the hurdles were over with, that he should concentrate on his job which was the source of financial sustenance of the family.

CHAPTER TEN

CAREER, A THIRD PARTY

A career is born out of a burning desire to fulfil a lifestyle, habit, or practice. The dictionary defines habit as, "A regular tendency to practice, especially one that is hard to give up. It is synonymous with custom, practice, pattern, norm and tradition." (Web dictionary)

Whatever goes wrong could be viewed as a mistake, a repeat of same is seen as a practice, a third performance of the same makes it a habit, and any repeat makes it a lifestyle. It is very difficult for any individual to break away from a lifestyle.

The Bible states,

""Can the Ethiopian change his skin Or the leopard his spots? Then you also can do good who are accustomed to evil and even trained to do it." JER. 13:23 AMP

Tina's father was a senior official of one of the foremost airlines in the United States of America. She was used to traveling because the family by right was entitled to what is called privilege-ticket for most of their traveling. She had always looked forward to the holiday seasons. Her father had tied her travels to her academic performance. She had the aspiration to top her class so that she could have a wonderful trip to a destination of her choice. She was adjudged by her teachers as the most brilliant student in the school. In most cases she scores straight A. If she scores anything lower than a "B" in any subject, the head teacher would review the performance of the teacher of the particular subject. She was the youngest student in her final year in college. She was voted to be the valedictorian at their graduation ceremony. She performed excellently well. She had a lot of job offers which were declined because the university offered her a scholarship for her postgraduate studies. Her research work was an eye-opener in the aviation industry. She got a good job that made her the aspiration of many. Marriage became the next thing in the plan of her father. He was anxious to have his daughter married and settle to have her own family.

Hugo was the topmost poet and novelist of his time. His fame and popularity was next to none. Tina had read many of his poems and novel in the course of her traveling to avoid boredom. She was anxious to meet with her most admired writer. Their meeting was a beautiful coincidence. They were seated next to each other on a flight to Frankfurt. Tina was reading one of the novels written by her unrecognized next neighbor. Interestingly, Hugo realized that she was reading one of his novels titled: "Romance with the Beast." He had watched the disposition of Tina and was in admiration of her beauty and composure. He could not find any easy way to get her attention as she glued her eyes to the narratives that had taken her out of the regular terrestrial world. He could not find any easier way than to introduce himself as the author of the obsessive novel that had cut her off any communication with her environment. Her countenance changed. It was a connection with a life dream. The discussion was very cordial. Hugo was very impressed by her given attention but thought it must all be connected only to her meeting him for the very first time. He was cautious not to assume she had any conjugal attachment to her expressions. She fell in love with him but could not speak her mind. She assessed his age and asked a very inquisitive question, "Are you married?" He responded in the characteristic styles of one of the characters in his novel,"I am still hunting." "Of a fact or of a cast?" Asked Tina with a smile. "Of a fact." Hugo asserted. They both smiled. Her face dropped as she looked at his face compared with the picture at the back of the novel as if to confirm the authenticity of his claim.

With a smile he said, "not the picture anymore but the real being. It is me." She gave him a hand shake for a good job as she decided to prove a little difficult not to sell herself cheap. The sensation of her cool smooth palm sent a sensation into Hugo's nerves. She withdrew to herself to continue her reading. She was actually not reading but thinking. Hugo was a little taken aback. He did not know what to do next. It was a complete switch. He reached for his carry-on bag and pulled out his latest novel. He turned to Tina and said, "Please add this to your collection, my business card is in one of the pages. It's a pleasure meeting you." Tina felt he was offended by her switch. She was not going to give him a wrong impression of herself. She responded, "You are very captivating in writing and in person. I was going to continue on the thriller in my hand. Thanks for the addition. She reached for her wallet and gave him a copy of her complimentary card. Hugo read through the content and was fascinated to get to know her better. The plane landed and they both had to rush out for their connecting flights.

The trip was one of the most impressive trips Tina ever had. She wished she had more time to freely relate with her most avowed author. She could not wait to share her experience with her mother who had always been her reading partner of Hugo's marvelous novels. She was waiting to board her flight when her phone rang. It was an unknown number. She was reluctant to pick the call but her imagination ran wild, she thought it could be a call from Hugo. It was a telemarketer. She almost punched the button off in anger as she hung up the phone. Shortly before her connecting flight took off, her phone rang again. She looked at the screen, it was an unknown number she declined the call. The phone rang again. She angrily picked the call but was silent. The caller was shy to talk but just said, "I am calling for Tina, my name is Hugo. She responded with excitement, "How are you, did you make your." The call was accidentally disconnected in error on her part. She looked at the handset as if it were to be demonic. She quickly redialed the number but to no avail. The announcement came that all electronics should be switched off as the plane was about to take off. It was a successful take off. Tina wished the take-off was a little delayed. She took the latest novel given to her by Hugo. She had another look of his picture. With a smile she soliloquized, "I wish we get together again." With her head dropped, she meditated that the Lord should make the heart of Hugo to pant after her. She invariably comforted herself that his heart was already panting after her. In her conclusions, that was the reason why he called. She could not read any of the novels but slept off in her thoughts of finding herself in the heart and arms of Hugo. The pilot did a good job to have landed the plane smoothly. Tina was woken up by the clap of hands by the passengers in appreciation of the pilot for a perfectly smooth landing.

She called her Mom to inform her of her safe landing at the Houston airport. Her mother responded that they were already at the airport awaiting her arrival. She told her mother that she was aboard same plane with their much celebrated Hugo. She went hysteric. "Gooood! I will get to meet him. Please keep his company as you come out of the plane." She could not tell her mother the details as she had to switch off her phone at the immigration counter. As she was walking out of the immigration section, she walked into an old classmate who came in another flight. They walked to the arrival door together. Her mom in her assumption believed that he was Mr. Hugo Vaughan. "With excitement she said, "Its nice meeting you, we have read many of your works..." "No mom, this is not Hugo, this is Brandy my high school mate. We met on arrival." "I am sorry, I was over excited to meet Hugo, and how I wish you brought him with you." Her mother responded. "I can always get him for you, he gave me his business card when we were about to part in Frankfort" "Is he interested in you..." "Ooh mom, why so soon..." "I just love him for his writing. He must be very diligent and averagely successful to have been in the business class with you. Was your ticket not of business class?" "I had an upgrade, we were in the first class." "Whaoo, he must be up there. Please bring him home, I will readily welcome him into the family."

Tina was already in love with Hugo if he ever chose to express interest in her. She was riding more on her mother's conviction especially because she had never approved of previous men who had shown conjugal interest in her. She was not going to call Hugo but was anxious to receive a call from him. The call came, it was the beginning of what culminated into a holy matrimony. Hugo had always desired to live in the United States of America. His relationship with Tina afforded him a green light and a green card that eventually made him a citizen of America by marriage. The relationship like every other had its challenges. They both had to spend time to under-stand their individual temperaments. They had to adjust to the differences in their career interests and challenges.

It was a big challenge for Tina to cut down on her traveling. She was addicted to tourism. She failed to realize that the days of privileged tickets from her father's job were over with. There was hardly anything her husband could do to stop her traveling.

He was not very much against her traveling as it afforded him more time to concentrate on his writing. The crux of it all was that Tina desired to always travel with her husband. She knew he was the admiration of many ladies. She was very jealous and protective of him.

The arrival of their first child slowed down the travel of Tina, however it did not work out right for Hugo. He felt disturbed and his writing career infringed upon by the desired attention of his wife and baby. He made a clever move for his wife to go on holiday with the baby. His plan failed as Tina insisted that they all had to go on the trip. Hugo was used to solitude, a practice that had turned out to be the bedrock of his successful career. He was a victim of oppression by his step mother. His relationship with his wife got strained. Hugo and his mother-in-law were always in perfect rapport. He approached her in tears expressing his fears that his career was at stake. He was not too impressed by the response of his mother-in-law. She was of the opinion that he got to take care of his family first. Hugo felt betrayed by his ardent reader and admirer whom he had taken to be a replacement of his biological mother. He sought the counsel of his father. Who told him he was obsessed by his carrier. He was reminded of the cause of conflicts between them both when he was in high school and college respectively. He spent most of his time in solitude, either reading or writing. He hardly would want to be involved in dialogue with his siblings. Major cause of conflicts in his youthful days was his negligence on the house chores. His father had warned him in anticipation of his married life. He was of the opinion that any undomesticated child will be a liability in marriage. He [Hugo] had not much confidence in his step mother whom he grew to know as his mother because his biological mother died at his birth. He sought the advice of a marriage counsellor, he was not happy with the counsel of the aging counselor. He felt the whole world was against him.

Hugo had very strong love and affection for his family but could not figure out how to manage his carrier and his family life. He felt like a fish out of water. In his impetus anger he called his wife and told her he would want a divorce or he would commit suicide. Tina could not in her wildest imagination think her husband had such a propensity. She was very scared, frustrated and unsecured. She rushed to meet her mom who had become her husband's greatest confidant. He had taken her to be his biological mother as he found solace in her, having struggled to outgrow the high handedness of his step mother. Grandma Justine was shocked by the information. She abandoned everything to attend to her very treasured son-in-law. While on their way she spoke passionately to her daughter that she needed to reconsider her approach to the relationship between her and her husband Hugo. She said, "My beloved daughter, please do not view your husband as heartless and suicidal. You know he has been a very affectionate and loving husband and a good father to his son. He really loves you and us all. I am sure he is just very frustrated because the source of his recognition, popularity and productivity came under a very serious attack since he got married to you..." Tina was furious at her mother's statement. "Am I the cause of his frustrations, when did I become a liability? Did he marry me or his hobby, habit and boring life style? I have been very tolerant and considerate in the past three years of this marriage. Haven't I reported to you in the past that he has little or no time for me? Our closest time was during our honeymoon which he terminated against our agreed plan all because he was to meet a deadline with his publisher. I do not want to marry a deadline man. I want to work with a lifeline. I am actually getting tired of his boredom. If he wants a divorce, I guess that will be better. He could then find a woman that will marry his boredom." Her mother was worst shocked more than ever. She exploded, "Am I hearing you or someone else? Tina... you do not want to become a single parent I believe. What is it that must have gone wrong with your Christian profession of faith? Have you backslidden into the worldly concept of marriage?" With tears, Tina subbed as she told her mother of her pains over the years. She felt she had no marriage. She claimed she had never wanted to share her pains and loneliness with anybody. Her believe was that almost everybody felt she was at the top of the world being the wife of a celebrated and best read poet and novelist of their time. She was very emotionally broken. Her mother advised she should park the car for her to take over the driving. She wiped her face, tried to comport herself as she determined to continue the driving. Her mother appealed to her understanding, she said, "It is interesting that your boredom is the source of excitement and joy to millions across the globe. " "No more will that be, I cannot afford to sacrifice my joy for the world." "But you enjoy their money for your boredom." Her mother asserted. She silently ruminated over her mother's convicting statement.

They arrived the home of Tina and Hugo Vaughan. Grandma was very happy to see that her beloved son-in-law was in the study. He was busy with his writing. He came into the sitting room to confirm it was his wife that came back into the house as she never told him about her movement after the very devastating threat of divorce or suicide. Grandma Justine apologized for the disturbance or interruption of his flow of thoughts as she herself knew that a disruption in the flow of expression may be very frustrating to a writer. Hugo was very receptive as he said, "Mom, I really need your presence, I am fed up with life. My publishers want me to meet the deadline, I am yet to meet-up with my publications for the journals. I am a week behind in my television presentations, all because I must create time to meet up with the family demands. If I knew marriage is this demanding, I would not have gotten into it." His mother-in-law cut in to say, "You have not made a mistake."

"The most painful aspect of it all is that my wife charged me for abandonment. I am tired of life. I love my wife and our only son which may always be. I am tired of obstructions to my life..." Tina was fuming but she knew any emotional outburst may worsen the issue at hand. She was just silent but could not hold back tears. She had her fears. She knew the world would blame her for any negative development. Hugo did not realize that his wife was in tears as she bowed her head. He was shocked when he realized she was actually sobbing. He pulled her to himself and said, "I guess I cannot handle this anymore, one of us got to go, to make the other happy. Grandma Justine was very scared. Tina was devastated. She hooted, "I don't know what else to do. Why must one of us have to go... go where?" "Die or divorce," he replied. Tina fell on the floor holding to the legs of her husband. Grandma Justine was torn between two walls. She held Hugo to her chest with a plea that there were more to life than the thoughts of divorce or suicide. He looked into her eyes and said, "What do I have to live for if I cannot fulfill purpose." Tina was ready to do anything to save her marriage and the life of her husband. She rose from the floor, went straight to her husband with a plea that she would do whatever he wanted at least to reassure him of life. Hugo was broken, he responded with tears as he said, "I never thought I will have to go through all these to keep myself together. If I knew that marriage is this demanding, I would not have gotten involved. I could not resist your personality, I thought your disposition and mine are very compatible. I love you but I do not know how to handle the situation. I do not talk about divorce based on hatred but a plan to keep my desired accomplishment. I will always love you even when we are divorced. With our son, you can never get out of my life." The word divorce was very traumatizing to Tina and her mother. Tina held her husband with a very stern look as she said, "Let's reach a compromise on this, I am ready to let you do your writing the way you want to have it. Let your time be at your disposal. You do not have to travel with us if you choose not to. I promise you my piety and fidelity. Be at liberty to demand sex at your convenience. I promise not to trouble you anymore for sex if you choose to be insensitive to my moves or passion. Please tell me what you need me to do so that you stay alive. You have made impact on many lives than you wasting your life because of your marriage to me. It could probably have been worse with any other woman. I guess I may not be the worst woman on the surface of the earth. Your death or divorce will invariably paint me and my parents black in the hearts of millions of people connected with you." Her appeal was halted by the sudden hoot of her husband. "I do not mean to put you through all these... why would you enslave yourself because of me?" "I will do anything possible to save your image and this marriage," he muttered. Hugo was completely shattered. He wept like a baby as he asked his wife, "Tell me what will make you happy." "That you choose to live and do whatever makes you happy. I have not come into your life to ruin you or terminate your purpose. Your wish shall be my command. Just let me know what gives you joy. I guess I know what gives you joy. I have determined to let you have the fullness of it," she emphatically reassured her husband. He was the more broken. He felt like giving his wife a kiss but could not agree in himself that the circumstance at hand will give it the true desired expression. He told his wife, "The best day of my life was the day I met you. You this day saved my life. I have had the premonition to end it tonight, you have just revitalized and invigorated my soul. I felt a renewal of zeal and strength to pursue my purpose in life. He pulled her to himself with a very passionate kiss. "I this day determine to live for you. I love you, you are my angel. You saved my life."

Grandma Justine was overwhelmed with joy. Tears of joy were rolling down her cheeks as she embraced them both. Hugo said. "Mom, you gave birth to me in France and disappeared to the USA for the birth of the only woman that has saved my life. Mom, I shall live to make you happy. Tina was completely flabbergasted by the development. She pulled her husband closer and gave him a very passionate kiss that made Grandma Justine nostalgic. She said, "I missed my husband..." It was a wonderful time of reunion. Tina reassured her husband that she will never obstruct him on his pursuit of his life ambition. He felt guilty. He responded with a promise, "Please do not think you have lost me to my lifelong habit. Please be my safety valve to keep me in the same world with the would be successful people. They promised each other to be reliable helpmates.

Hugo, contrary to his usual practice offered to give his mother-in-law a ride back to her residence. She declined all because she wanted to have time with her daughter in the course of their trip back to her home. She really appreciated him for his kind gesture. She humorously said; "if you agreed to stop your writing to give me a ride home, I feel like I'm on top of the world. The gesture is enough. I would have accepted the ride but I need to talk with your wife in the course of the ride." "Please beg her on my behalf." To his wife he said, "I shall not die but live to declare the goodness of the Lord in the land of the living. I can never do without you my angel." With a smile she gave him a hug as she picked the car key. Hugo went back into his study while Tina took his mother back to her home. As they drove off, grandma Justine touched the shoulder of her daughter as she said, "Was king Solomon not right when he said, *"Do not rush out to argue your case [before magistrates or judges]; Otherwise what will you do in the end [when your case is lost and] When your neighbor (opponent) humiliates you? Argue your case with your neighbor himself [before you go to court]; and do not reveal another's secret, Or he who hears it will shame you And the rumor about you [and your action in court] will have no end. Like apples of gold in settings of silver is a word spoken at the right time.""* She read from the Holy Bible PROVERBS 25:8-11 AMP.

Tina was very appreciative of her mother. She said, "Mom, you saved my husband and my marriage." "The Lord did. It was a divine intervention. I am proud of you. You did all I was going to appeal to you to do to save your marriage and more so the life of your husband." Her mother responded. "Mom, I am happy my husband has very high regard for you. He really sees you as his mother." "He will surely believe that his assertions were right that I came to give birth to his wife in America." They both laughed. "I am happy I got my husband back." Her mother was of the opinion that she upgrades her care for him. She said, "May I suggest that his meals should not fail, I am sure you are aware that he is not too concerned about his appearance. Make sure you fix his dresses and get him to trim his beards and mustache. Check his hair cut..." "Mom, you do not realize that I need someone to take care of me too. Now that you made me have two children." "Are you pregnant?" Her mother questioned. Not that I know of but for your new big-boy Hugo." They both laughed. "Mom, I promise to exceed your expectations. I am going to actually get involved with him on his writings. One of my plans is to get him to publish his books on his own named company. It shall be called HUGO PUBLISHING HOUSE. I have already secured a domain for HUGO.COM." "That is a brilliant idea, please assure him that I will be ready to offer free services for the effective take off of the company."

Tina returned home to a radiant husband. She fixed his dinner and invited him to table. He was about to round-off a story line so he delayed in his response to her invitation. On his arrival he knew that his wife was not pleased for the fact that he delayed in his response. He apologized as he said, "Come to think of it, I was just writing about my new found love for you. The fact remains that the public sees the glamor, the celebration of grand moments in the lives of the celebrities without a clue to the trauma and torture suffered by people in their private life. If you wouldn't mind let me read a poem I just wrote in appreciation of your love." "After you have finished the meal," she insisted. It was bedtime, Tina was too tired to listen to any poem. She had had a very challenging and busy time with the chores around the house coupled with her care for "Junior" their only son. She realized she promised to hear the poem after he had eaten the meal. She gathered some strength as she said to her husband. "I guess your poem will play a better role than any sleep tablet. He was very excited, he rushed back into his study to fetch his laptop. He read:

"He was drowning in the waves of habits,

She was drawing up a plan of rescue,

Neither to drown him nor his habits,

She saw the waves as a recourse,

A rabbit that was biting on the habit,

The challenge was her required course.

She planned to sacrifice the rabbit for the habit,

Life was ebbing out on him until her recourse.

Now the rabbit could not stop the habit.

Life continues with her recourse.

She was the source of life in the habit,

Her habit became a recourse

The habits were rescued not the rabbit.

Tina my angel, her recourse rescued my habit."

She listened with rapt attention, she felt very excitedly happy. She slept off on his chest after a fill of her pleasure. Deep down in her heart, she desired that the pleasure should give her another treasure. Joy was restored and happiness permeated the aura of the family.

Further Reading

1. Tim. LaHaye—- Spirit Controlled Temperament.
2. Walter Trohisch —- I married You.
3. John Lane. An internet posting Dec. 8th 1998. Feast of the immaculate conception home. Scanned and proofed by Mark Mansfield.

Hhttp://www.angelicum.net/html/four_temperaments.html

1. The Holy Bible. King James Version.
2. The Holy Bible: The American Standard Version.
3. The Holy Bible: The Amplified Version.

Decision Page

I want to invite you to make Jesus your Lord and personal savior if you have not done so. Boycott Hell and embrace eternal life given through believing in Jesus as your Lord and personal savior. Prayer and fasting will not work if you do not belong to the kingdom of God, and if you don't with sincerity of heart declare for Jesus. If today, you agree to give your life to Jesus, the sample prayer below will change your life and relationship for the better. God is the author of marriage, He will give you the best of it.

Please pray:
Dear Jesus, I believe you died for me and that you rose again on the third day. I confess to you that I am a sinner and that I need your love and forgiveness. Come into my life, forgive my sins, and turn my life around. With my mouth I confess that you are the son of God. In my heart I believe that God raised you from the dead. I declare that you are my Lord and Master. Thank You Jesus. From today, help me to walk in your peace, love, forgiveness and joy forever.

Signed: _____

Date: _____

Call for counseling or ministration
Contact me at: 832-723-8470

About the Author

Pastor Ade Okonrende is the product of the union between Samuel Akinlabi and Henrietta Ojuolape Okonrende nee Adeseolu. They both hailed from Abeokuta, Ogun State, Nigeria.

Samuel Okonrende became a polygamist with four wives. It was his plan just to train the first male child of each of the wives. This gave Ade little or no chance to higher education because he was the second surviving male child of his mother. His mother very much valued education. It was her determination that afforded all her children the attainment of appreciable academic qualifications.

Ade Okonrende is an alumnus of the UNIVERSITY OF IFE now OBAFEMI AWOLOWO UNIVERSITY, Ile-Ife, Nigeria and THE REDEEMED CHRISTIAN BIBLE COLLEGE, London. He pioneered The RCCG in the

United Kingdom; 1990-1999 before he relocated to USA with his family in 1999. He was the protagonist of RCCG in France. His family ministry was officially launched in London in 1995 in commemoration of ten years of marriage

Along with his wife they have published many books and over one hundred thousand pamphlets (Family Issues) on Christian Marriage.

He is a Regional Pastor in the RCCG North America. He is directly in-charge of peace and reconciliation. As at the time of publishing this book served as the Senior Pastor of RCCGNA Pavilion of Redemption, 15227 Old Richmond Road, Sugarland, Texas USA.

His marriage is blessed with four children: Grace, Chosen, Choice and Royal (RCCG) and increasing grandchildren to the glory of God.

Notes

Made in the USA
Columbia, SC
01 November 2021